W. G. SEBALD

W. G. SEBALD

Uwe Schütte

NORTHCOTE

BRITISH COUNCIL

© 2018 by Uwe Schütte

Quotations and images by W. G. Sebald. © 2018, The Estate of W. G. Sebald, used by permission of The Wylie Agency (UK) Limited.

First published in 2018 by
Liverpool University Press
4 Cambridge Street
Liverpool L69 7ZU

on behalf of
Northcote House Publishers Ltd
Mary Tavy
Devon PL19 9PY

British Library Cataloguing-in-Publication Data
A catalogue record for this book is available from the British Library

ISBN 978-0-7463-1298-8 hardcover
ISBN 978-0-7463-1299-5 paperback

Typeset by PDQ Typesetting, Newcastle-under-Lyme
Printed and bound by CPI Group (UK) Ltd, Croydon, CR0 4YY

Contents

Illustrations

1. The modernist architecture of the University of East Anglia (© N. Chadwick)
2. Sebald's beloved grandfather Josef Egelhofer (Deutsches Literaturarchiv, The Wiley Agency)
3. Old Rectory in Poringland, Norfolk (Jo Catling)
4. Sebald in Stuttgart, 2001 (Heiner Wittman)
5. Manchester chimneys, photographed by Sebald (The Wylie Agency)
6. Obituary of Armin Müller
7. Photograph taken by Walter Genewein of three women in the ghetto Litzmannstadt (The Jewish Museum, Frankfurt)
8. Storm devastation in 1987, photograph taken by Sebald (The Wylie Agency)

Acknowledgements

This general introduction to the life and works of W. G. Sebald aims to provide an English-speaking audience with a deeper understanding of the complexities behind one of the most compelling and original literary voices of the late twentieth century.

The picture of Sebald painted in this small study is inevitably influenced by my personal acquaintance with him. I arrived at the University of East Anglia in the autumn of 1992, having read only his first work of prose, *Schwindel. Gefühle.* (translated *Vertigo*). While I did both my MA and PhD qualification with him from 1992 to 1997 as his sole post-graduate student at the time, I could witness his meteoric rise to international literary fame from a close distance.

Sebald greatly differed from the professors at German universities as he actively fostered a close relationship between supervisor and student. He asked for my opinion on unpublished critical texts and coyly accepted praise for his literary books. Always modest, friendly and helpful I found him to be an extraordinary exception in literary circles consisting very often of self-important academics and egotistical writers.

This study attempts no hagiography but aims at a critical evaluation of Sebald's works. By doing this, it sets out to rectify various myths and distortions that govern the perception of this unique writer. A writer, who was not only caught between two cultures but was equally stuck between outsider status and canonization, the demands of academia and the world of literature.

Sebald's *œuvre* will be discussed in the order in which his books were published in Germany to provide a deeper understanding of the original development of his works. Also, I will look at Sebald's critical writings, which were written over three decades and often fed into his literary texts. Even though Sebald's collected work is comparatively small, not every aspect of his rich and complex writings can be discussed here. Readers with a command of German are referred to my various monographs on Sebald, ranging from a general introduction to the comprehensive study of his critical writings and a more concise overview of his poetry, as well as an edited volume which focuses on neglected aspects of the works.

I am grateful to Brian Hulme for the invitation to contribute to this series and thereby convincing me to tackle my first book in English. Over the years, Jo Catling, Sven Meyer, Scott Bartsch, Richard Sheppard, Iain Galbraith, Christian Wirth and Peter Oberschelp supported me in various ways in all things Sebald. Melissa Etzler greatly helped with archive matters and spotted many oversights.

Referring to his command of the English language, Sebald on one occasion maintained that 'I don't in the least feel at home in it. I use it but it sounds quite alien to me' (*CB* 148). Regrettably, the same applies to me. Scott Bartsch, Adrian West, Melissa Etzler, Jenny Price and Antje Blank came to my help. Sina Rahmani in particular was indispensable for ironing out my many linguistic deficiencies and converting meandering sentences to readable English. Particular credits go to him for this arduous task as well as for the advice, he gave (even though I occasionally ignored it). Ute Sebald allowed me to quote from her late husband's papers kept at the Deutsches Literaturarchiv (DLA) in Marbach am Neckar.

Final thanks, as always, go to my wife, Antje. She always supported me to find the time for writing this book at the expense of spending my time with her and our son, Lenz.

Biographical Outline

1944   Born Winfried Georg Sebald on 18 May (Ascension Day) in Wertach, Allgäu (Bavaria).

1947   Return of father Georg Sebald from POW camp in France.

1952   Family moves to nearby Sonthofen where father worked for local police as a locksmith.

1956   Death of grandfather Josef Egelhofer. Father joins newly established *Bundeswehr* (federal army) as an officer.

1962   Attends screening of film about the liberation of Belsen at school.

1963   Admitted to the University of Freiburg where he studies German and English literature.

1965   Transfers to the Université de Fribourg (Switzerland). Stays with sister Gertrud Aebischer-Sebald.

1966   Receives his Fribourg *licence ès lettres* for dissertation on Carl Sternheim. Appointed as language teaching assistant (*Lektor*) at the University of Manchester.

1967   Writes to T. W. Adorno with query regarding Sternheim. Marriage in Sonthofen.

1968   Presents MA dissertation on Sternheim at University of Manchester. Teaches German and English in an international boarding school in St Gallen (Switzerland). Unsuccessfully applies for Junior Research Fellowship at Sidney Sussex College, Cambridge.

1969   *Carl Sternheim: Kritiker und Opfer der Wilhelminischen Ära* (revised version of MA dissertation) published. Returns to Manchester reappointed as *Lektor*.

1970   Rejects post in the Drama Department of the University of Bangor. Appointed to Assistant Lectureship in German Language and Literature at the

	University of East Anglia (UEA), Norwich. Rents flat in Wymondham, Norfolk.
1971	Moves into own house in Wymondham. Works on PhD thesis on Alfred Döblin.
1973	Submits PhD thesis on Döblin (in English). Promoted to Lectureship.
1974	Receives PhD. Presents paper at Kafka conference organized at UEA.
1975	Successfully applies for training course as language teacher at the Goethe-Institute. Sells house in Wymondham.
1976	Attends teacher training course in Munich but decides to withdraw. Returns to the UK. Purchase of dilapidated Old Rectory in Poringland.
1980	*Der Mythus der Zerstörung im Werk Döblins* (revised German version of PhD thesis) published. Visits mentally ill artists in the Lower Austrian Psychiatric Institution at Gugging and befriends the schizophrenic poet Ernst Herbeck.
1981	Interviews Solly Zuckerman on the Second World War area bombing campaign. Travels to New York to take part in Döblin conference. Visits relatives in New Jersey.
1982	Publication of essay addressing the literary representation of the area bombing of Germany.
1985	*Die Beschreibung des Unglücks* (essay collection on Austrian literature) published. Promoted to Senior Lecturer.
1987	Travels through northern Italy – Venice, Limone, Milan (where a new passport is issued by the German Consulate), Verona. Chairs a conference on Contemporary German Drama at UEA. Promoted to Reader.
1988	*Nach der Natur (After Nature)* published. Promoted to Professor of European Literature.
1989	Foundation of the British Centre for Literary Translation (BCLT) at UEA. Assumes position as Director.
1990	*Schwindel. Gefühle. (Vertigo)* published. Takes part in the Ingeborg Bachmann-Prize in Klagenfurt (Austria) with public reading of *Paul Bereyter* story from *The Emigrants* but is snubbed by jury.

1991   *Unheimliche Heimat* (essay collection on Austrian literature) published. Receives Fedor Malchow Prize for *After Nature* in Hamburg.

1992   *Die Ausgewanderten (The Emigrants)* published.

1993   *The Emigrants* is discussed on German TV in programme *Das Literarische Quartett*. Makes individual trips to various parts of East Anglia later featuring in *The Rings of Saturn*. Admitted to Norfolk and Norwich Hospital for a back operation.

1994   Receives Berlin Literature Prize / Johannes Bobrowski Medal. Throws medal in the Kleiner Wannsee near the grave of Heinrich von Kleist. Awarded LiteraTour Nord Prize.

1995   *Die Ringe des Saturn (The Rings of Saturn)* published. Travels to Corsica in connection with research for a book on the island.

1996   Elected member of Deutsche Akademie für Sprache und Dichtung (German Academy of Language and Literature). Travels again to Corsica but later abandons the Corsica Project, parts of which posthumously appear in *Campo Santo*.

1997   Delivers three controversial lectures in Zurich on air war and literature. Receives Mörike Prize in Fellbach, Heinrich Böll Prize in Cologne and *Jewish Quarterly/Wingate Prize for Literature* in London.

1998   *Logis in einem Landhaus (A Place in the Country)* published.

1999   *Luftkrieg und Literatur (The Natural History of Destruction)* published. Visits Prague, Terezín and Nuremberg. Death of father. He is transferred from School of Modern Languages and European Studies to School of English and American Studies at UEA.

2000   Awarded NESTA (National Endowment for Science, Technology and the Arts) Fellowship. Teaches creative writing to MA students at UEA. Receives Heinrich Heine Prize in Düsseldorf and Joseph Breitbach Prize in Mainz.

2001   *For Years Now* and *Austerlitz* published. Dies on 14 December of aneurysm while driving near his home. Buried in St Andrew's Churchyard, Framingham Earl.

2002   National Book Critic's Circle Award, Bremen Literary

Prize and Wingate Literary Prize, all awarded post-humously for *Austerlitz*.

A far more extensive chronology by Richard Sheppard can be found in *Saturn's Moons*. It also aligns these biographical dates with the fictional ones given for the narrator in his literary texts.

Abbreviations and References

I have used the widely available UK paperback editions of Sebald's works. Translations from German texts unavailable in English are my own.

A	*Austerlitz* (London: Penguin, 2002)
ALW	*Across the Land and the Water* (London: Penguin, 2012)
AN	*After Nature* (London: Penguin, 2003)
CS	*Campo Santo* (Penguin, 2006)
E	*The Emigrants* (London: Vintage, 2002)
NHD	*On the Natural History of Destruction* (London: Penguin, 2004)
PC	*A Place in the Country* (London: Penguin, 2014)
RS	*The Rings of Saturn* (London: Vintage, 2002)
V	*Vertigo* (London: Vintage, 2002)
CB	'In Conversation with W. G. Sebald', in: *Writers in Conversation with Christopher Bigsby*, ed. Christopher Bigsby, vol. 2 (Norwich: EAS Publishing/Pen & Inc, 2001), 139–65
EM	*The Emergence of Memory: Conversations with W. G. Sebald*, ed. Lynne Sharon Schwartz (New York: Seven Stories, 2007)
SM	*Saturn's Moons: W. G. Sebald – A Handbook*, ed. Jo Catling & Richard Hibbitt (Oxford: Legenda, 2011)

1

W. G. Sebald: Emigrant and Academic

'I do like to be on the margins if possible.'

(Sebald in conversation with Eleanor Wachtel)

Winfried Georg Sebald both began and ended his life on the periphery. Born in the waning days of the Second World War in a very rural corner of South Germany, the angry young man left his fatherland at a time when the impact of Nazi values was still felt in German society. That also applied to the University of Freiburg where he read German and English literature: 'When I began my own studies,' the narrator in *Austerlitz* explains, 'I had learnt almost nothing from the scholars then lecturing in the humanities there, most of them academics who had built their careers in the 1930s and 1940s and still nurtured delusions of power' (*A* 43). Sebald did not tolerate this, as he felt, deeply deplorable situation and he decided to expatriate himself.

First, he went to the French-speaking part of Switzerland to complete his BA at the Université de Fribourg. From this picturesque medieval town Sebald moved on to the grimy industrial city of Manchester in 1966. He was shocked by his new environs: 'I thought I had arrived on another planet and it took me a long time to get used to it. The experience cast me in a considerable depression which lasted until Christmas' (*CB* 149), he later recollected. Sebald's first venture to England barely lasted two years. After a sojourn back in Switzerland, where he spent an unhappy academic year as a teacher of German at a private boarding school, he returned to Manchester at the end of the Sixties to start work on his doctorate. Sebald was determined to start a career as an academic in England, and

1

Illustration 1: The modernist architecture
of the University of East Anglia

he succeeded: in 1970 he earned a teaching position at the
University of East Anglia (UEA) in Norwich. Little could he have
known at the time that he would eventually spend his entire
academic career at UEA.

First, it seemed as if all was going to plan. Sebald spent happy
years working in the progressive, recently founded institution.
But the situation at the university worsened because of the many
reforms that were increasingly introduced by inept politicians
following neoliberal agendas. His escape from the pressures and
demands of his academic job took the form of an increasing
interest in literary writing. In 1988, Sebald's career achieved two
milestones. With the publication of *After Nature* in the late
summer, he formally turned into a literary writer, and, in October
of that year, he was promoted to a chair in European Literature.

From this point on, Sebald's career consisted of two parallel
tracks: he was both professor of literature and writer of
literature. During the 1990s, he produced polemic essays
attacking German writers as well as extraordinary pieces of
fiction that quickly elevated him to international fame. However,
fame brought a new set of pressures and demands. During the
second half of the decade, Sebald's outlook on life became

increasingly darker as his physical state of health worsened. Having reached the apex of his career in 2001 with the publication of *Austerlitz* in both German and English, Sebald died while driving near his home. He was only 57 years old.

*

That much for a short version of Sebald's biography. But his life warrants a closer look. Many details have come to light since his death in December 2001. Interviews with biographical information have become more easily accessible, memoirs by friends and colleagues are being published, eager academics have unearthed unknown material from his estate, and avid readers of his books have lovingly compiled information about his life and works. Despite all of this, Sebald continues to evade us, and it is doubtful whether this will ever truly change. He guarded his private life vigorously. And indeed, it is not really necessary to know every detail of Sebald's biography in order to appreciate his extraordinary works. Nevertheless, an awareness of the decisive biographical events and the underlying issues that influenced his approach to literature is indispensable for a better understanding of his books. That concerns in particular two related aspects of which many Sebald readers have limited knowledge – namely the vast body of critical writings and his struggle against the restructuring of British Higher Education.[1]

Near the end of the 1990s, Sebald tried to extricate himself from his teaching and administrative obligations. And, as it happened, he did find a way out: in 2000 he received a £73,000 grant from the National Endowment for Science, Technology and the Arts (NESTA) that would have allowed him to teach only one term per year until his scheduled retirement in 2004, freeing up valuable time for researching and writing his next book after *Austerlitz*.[2] One of the questions on the application form asked, 'How do your achievements so far demonstrate that you have the attributes that we are seeking?' Sebald's response was an apt assertion that shines a helpful light on both his life and career: 'I was always determined to find my own way.'

*

Sebald was indeed born 'on Ascension Day/of the year forty-four' (*AN* 86) in Wertach, a village in rural Allgäu inhabited at that time by fewer than a thousand souls. His childhood during

3

the 1940s and 1950s later reminded him more of the conditions of pre-modern life. Sebald stressed the remoteness of the place, as well as the primitive way of life in the Alpine village, which was often covered in snow for five months a year. As a child, he remembered, he did not see any cars or other modern machinery. But something else was missing as well:

> There was scarcely any reading material about.... There was no bookshop; there was not even a local lending library or anything of that kind; you grew up without reading. And you grew up without listening to music..... Nobody had a gramophone; there was scarcely a radio. (*CB* 140–1)

Truly primitive conditions, which are a measure of how far he had to come before achieving fame as a writer. This also applies to his mastery of language; his 'native tongue' was the heavy thick dialect spoken in that south-western corner of Bavaria, which meant that he first had to learn 'proper' German in school. Later, he placed traces of this 'minor' language in his finely crafted literary German as a subversive assault on the laws of High German (something, it should be added, that is difficult to render in English and inevitably has been lost in translation).

But this is not the only hidden connection between his celebrated books and his upbringing in the backwaters of Germany. For example, his highlighting of the social and economic underdevelopment in the Allgäu region resulted in his sensitivity to 'the inequality or the unevenness of time' (*CB* 141), which in turn fed into speculations such as those of Austerlitz, who wondered whether 'time did not exist at all, only various spaces interlocking according to the rules of a higher form of stereometry' (*A* 261). Sebald's stubborn luddite worldview – although he did at least make use of telephones, fax machines and photocopiers – harks back to his idyllic, possibly paradise-like childhood that he felt expelled from in later years. 'Being surrounded by machines makes me panic' (*CB* 140) he once confessed.

Mark Anderson has unearthed many particulars pertaining to Sebald's familial background (see *SM* 16–37). For instance, three of his uncles and aunts were forced to emigrate for economic reasons to the United States in the 1920s, and fictional versions of the departures were used in 'Ambros Adelwarth', the third of the four stories in *The Emigrants*. Sebald himself followed in their footsteps when he left Germany for an academic career in the United Kingdom. Both his sisters emigrated from Germany, too. The experience of loss of *Heimat* is an important part of the Sebald family's experience. Sebald himself characterized his family roots thus:

> I come from a very conventional, Catholic, anti-Communist background. The kind of semi-working class, petit bourgeois background typical of those who supported the fascist regime, who went into the war not just blindly, but with a degree of enthusiasm. (*EM* 66)

The link he makes between sociological class and loyalty to fascism is a direct reference to one of the most important sociological axioms of the Frankfurt School, which had a major impact on Sebald's development as an intellectual. His statement also points to the life-long quarrel with his parents stemming from his dogmatic insistence that they were complicit with National Socialism (thereby implicating them in the crimes committed). 'I always try to explain to my parents that there is no difference between passive resistance and passive collaboration – it's the same thing. But they cannot understand that' (*EM* 67). Evidently, his decision to pursue an academic career, as well as the content of his writing, both critical and literary, were driven by a desire to distance himself from this morally poisoned 'family inheritance' which he perceived as a guilt he wanted to exorcise.

Closely connected to this is what Sebald described as the 'conspiracy of silence' regarding events during the Nazi era. His family, as Sebald knew very well, was representative of the general situation in post-war Germany in the way they dealt with the recent past. 'I cannot imagine my parents, for instance, ever talking about these matters between themselves. It was just a taboo zone which you didn't enter' (*EM* 44), he explained. 'Your parents never told you anything about their experiences because there was at the least a great deal of shame attached to these experiences. So one kept them under lock and seal' (*EM* 84–5). Conquering this deeply inscribed as well as widespread oblivion wasn't Sebald's sole mission; most of his post-war generation participated in this redemptive project that culminated in the student revolt of the late 1960s.

To describe his parents as Nazis, however, would be utterly misleading. What amplified the generational strain was the fact that Sebald's father had served in three armies as a professional soldier: he first enlisted in the *Reichswehr* during the last years of the Weimar Republic, then served in Hitler's *Wehrmacht* (participating in the Polish campaign), and later joined the newly established *Bundeswehr* in 1955. Georg Sebald therefore embodied, to his son, the calamitous tradition of German militarism, making relations between them difficult for much of Sebald's life. Yet his father was politically a liberal, and therefore at odds with the staunchly conservative climate in southern Bavaria. As a member of the Social Democratic Party, he served on the Sonthofen local town council for six years. And, as Sebald's colleague Chris Bigsby explains, 'the death of his father left him feeling exposed. For all his problematic relation to him, years later he still missed this man with whom he had felt at odds. There was, he confessed, a hole in his universe'.[3]

What had also hampered the relations between father and son from an early age was Georg Sebald's belated return from the war. A prisoner of war in France until 1947, the elder Sebald had no contact with his young son during the first three years of his life. The man who took up the role of father figure was Sebald's maternal grandfather, Josef Egelhofer. Sebald was extremely close to Egelhofer, closer than to anyone else. 'Egelhofer not only filled the space left by an absent father,' Anderson observes, 'he also represented an intelligent, forgiving, non-military kind of authority that formed such a marked contrast with Sebald's soldier father, a stickler for order and discipline' (*SM* 32). Together they went on long walks through the countryside. Egelhofer taught his grandson about animals, plants, herbs and all the tiny wonders of nature that meant so much to Sebald throughout his life. From him, Sebald also adopted his *Weltanschauung* based on an idiosyncratic philosophy of nature: Sebald was sternly anticlerical; he vehemently rejected the Catholic Church, in which he was raised, in particular, and Christian religion in general. He was, nevertheless, a militant believer in the transcendent, leaning towards a broadly-defined pantheism. This was complemented by a lifelong interest in metaphysics that had evident repercussions in his literary works.

Illustration 2: Sebald's beloved grandfather Josef Egelhofer

Egelhofer died in April 1956, shortly before Sebald turned twelve, an insurmountable loss for Sebald that reverberated throughout his life: 'As a boy I felt quite protected. His death when I was 12 wasn't something I ever quite got over. It brought an early awareness of mortality and that the other side of life is something horrendously empty.'[4] Just as fictional characters like Austerlitz, Henry Selwyn or Paul Bereyter, whose early traumas of prosecution return towards the end of their lives, from the mid 1990s Sebald became increasingly haunted by Egelhofer's death. In a short poem written in the year of his own death, he links the business of literary writing with the shocking early experience of seeing the body:

The smell

of my writing paper
puts me in mind
of the woodshavings
in my grandfather's
coffin[5]

Egelhofer, who was born in 1872, introduced Sebald to the nineteenth century and sparked his interest in writers like Adalbert Stifter, Robert Walser, Gottfried Keller, and Johann Peter Hebel. They all came from, broadly speaking, the same south-western part of the German-speaking territories and wrote in the same antiquated language that Egelhofer spoke. Also, the rather unmodish moustache that Sebald sported even as a young man is an obvious homage to his late grandfather, from whom he inherited a moustache brush he used throughout his life.[6] The two men shared, however, a far more important physical connection: Egelhofer, who lived to the age of 83, suffered from a heart defect that most probably exempted him from the First World War. Decades later, Sebald escaped obligatory military service in the Federal Republic for the same reason. This heart defect, in all likelihood, killed him when he suffered an aneurysm while driving outside Norwich in December 2001.

Sebald's fascination for the realm of the dead and the spectral, evident throughout his works, stems primarily from the loss of his beloved guardian and teacher. 'My interest in the departed, which has been fairly constant, comes from the moment of losing someone you couldn't really afford to lose' (*EM* 171), he once acknowledged. And it is in this sense that Sebald can be described as a 'ghost writer', haunted by the memory of his grandfather. The death of Egelhofer undoubtedly constitutes this disturbing primal scene in Sebald's life. 'I remember very well how, as a child, I stood for the first time by an open coffin, with the dull sense in my breast that my grandfather, lying there on wood shavings, had suffered a shameful injustice that none of us survivors could make good.' The resulting 'burden of grief' (*CS* 33) that Sebald bore for the

8

rest of his life, however, has often been all too carelessly attributed only to his mourning of genocidal crimes perpetrated by National Socialism. While these too were, of course, 'a shameful injustice that none of us survivors could make good', one should be very cautious indeed not to confuse the two.

Notwithstanding this caution, it goes without saying that the colossal catastrophe of National Socialism loomed large over his life. The way in which Sebald felt implicated in the atrocities, he once described as follows:

> While I was sitting in my pushchair and being wheeled through flowering meadows by my mother, the Jews of Corfu were being deported on a four-week trek to Poland. It is the simultaneity of a blissful childhood and these horrific events that now strikes me as quite incomprehensible. I know now that these things cast a very long shadow over my life.... While I don't feel any responsibility, I do feel a sense of shame. (*CB* 144)

With the express caution required when advancing a psycho-analytical hypothesis, I would like to suggest that the shocking first encounter with the Holocaust that Sebald experienced as a teenager could have functioned as what Sigmund Freud calls a 'screen memory' (*Deckerinnerung*) of the traumatic loss of Egelhofer. Finding the loss of his grandfather far too painful to deal with, the confrontation with the horrifying crimes committed by the Germans functioned as a substitute shielding the earlier trauma. In any case, Sebald's first confrontation with the Shoah occurred in a surreal manner and was an experience which evidently overwhelmed the emotional capacities of the teenager:

> Until I was about sixteen or seventeen, I really had heard practically nothing about the history that preceded the date of 1945. A period from 1933 to 1945 I never heard of, as the history curriculum at school didn't cater for this ... and when we were about seventeen we were confronted at school ... with one of those documentary films. I think it was the opening of Belsen Camp, without comment and without further ado. So there it was, and somehow, you know, we had to get our minds around it, which of course we didn't.[7]

*

Sebald was eight years old when his family moved from the village of Wertach to the small city of Sonthofen, some twelve miles away, where his father worked at a police station at the time. Later, Georg Sebald would serve in the army again and was stationed in a barracks located in the *Ordensburg*, a massive, fortress-like building built during the 1930s, originally intended by the Nazis as an élite school for training future generations of fervent National Socialists.

As soon as Sebald completed his secondary school education, he enrolled at the University of Freiburg, situated roughly 150 miles away from Sonthofen. From autumn 1963 to summer 1965, he studied German literature and English, an experience he did not recall with particular fondness later in life. In addition to the overcrowded lectures and underfunded libraries, he detested the academic staff: 'They'd all done their doctorates in the 1930s and 1940s. And of course they were all democrats. Except that it later emerged that they were all ardent supporters of the Nazi regime in one way or another' (*EM* 65). As unhappy as he was during this time, it was a period of profound importance to his career. Firstly, it was at university that Sebald made his 'debut' as a literary writer, publishing a number of short prose pieces and poems in the university's student magazine. It was towards the end of his student years that Sebald began to call himself Max as he disliked his given name Winfried since it sounded too Germanic.

His four semesters of study in Freiburg coincided with the Frankfurt Auschwitz trials, which, according to Sebald, were

the first public acknowledgement that there was such a thing as an unresolved German past.... I read the newspaper reports every day and they suddenly shifted my vision.... I understood that I had to find my own way through that maze of the German past and not be guided by those in teaching positions at that time. (*CB* 146–7)

Seeking out untainted intellectual guidance, he gravitated towards thinkers like Theodor W. Adorno, Walter Benjamin, Ernst Bloch, Max Horkheimer and Herbert Marcuse. What eventually came to be called Critical Theory, which was developed by these philosophers, the majority of whom were Jewish, was certainly no part of the curriculum at Freiburg. Sebald adopted the critical philosophy of the Frankfurt School long before it eventually became the intellectual foundation of the West German student revolt in the late 1960s.

Intellectually armed with Critical Theory, Sebald left Germany for the first time in 1965 when he moved to Fribourg in French-speaking Switzerland. Staying with his elder sister, Gertrud, he quickly learned French and joined the local university for one year. Since this was long before international student exchange programmes were as ubiquitous as they are today, his move was a very unusual decision. It offered Sebald the chance not only to leave behind his unloved *alma mater* but also complete his BA dissertation (*mémoire de licence*) in just one year. A sixty-page typescript – awkwardly entitled *Zu Carl Sternheim: Kritischer Versuch einer Orientierung über einen umstrittenen Autor (On Carl Sternheim: A Critical Attempt to Come to Terms with a Controversial Author)* – gained Sebald a *licence ès lettres* in July 1966, his first university qualification. But he did not stop there. Sebald wanted to carry on both with his dissertation on the Wilhelmine playwright Sternheim, as well as with studies abroad. He applied to the German Department at the University of Manchester for a position as a language assistant – and, to his surprise, was accepted. For the second time, Sebald emigrated to a country whose language he did not really speak and about which he knew little: 'I certainly had no idea of the history or the culture of this country, or of its topography. I knew nothing about the north/south divide or any of the other great English myths' (*CB* 149).

The move had mixed results. His arrival in Manchester was at once a shock and a liberation. The decaying, soot-ridden cradle of English industrialization was quite unlike anything that Sebald had hitherto experienced in his life. Although the literary accounts of his arrival in Manchester in *After Nature* and *The Emigrants* are fictionalized in several respects, the amazement and disbelief they convey about the urban degradation Sebald unexpectedly encountered are all too real. Nevertheless, at the university he found a highly congenial atmosphere:

> England had so much to offer in those days to aspiring young scholars, things which to me were quite out of the ordinary. I had a heated office. I could go to the library at any time and pretty much all the books that I wanted were there.... At the university there wasn't anything that resembled an authoritarian structure. For someone who had grown up in a system of this sort and who, by nature, has perhaps something of an anarchist streak, this really felt

like freedom. The freedom to follow my own designs was an extremely positive aspect. (*CB* 149–50)

Eminently liked by the senior staff in the German department, Sebald successfully applied for an extension of his year-long appointment. One professorial colleague described him as being 'so very German in his rejection of things German' while displaying a 'preference for the oddities and eccentricities of English life'.[8]

Alongside his academic work, Sebald continued his literary writing by working on an autobiographical novel that remains unpublished. While this early work contains a number of interesting motifs and themes that appear here for the first time, it betrays little of what was to come in his later prose works in terms of literary style. Some patterns of his mature prose fiction that occur in this early text are forms of bricolage and occasional breaks in time (such as flashbacks to the narrator's childhood); one also sees important themes such as nature and generational conflict. His main project, however, was the expansion of the Fribourg *mémoire* into an MA dissertation. Submitted successfully to Manchester University in March 1968, it was now nearly four times as long, comprising over 220 pages. This version received yet another, major post-submission revision in the Swiss town of St Gallen where Sebald went once his second year at Manchester had come to an end. Sebald spent an unhappy year in Switzerland from 1968 to 1969, working as a teacher at an expensive private boarding school while hoping for better times to come.

*

The prestigious Kohlhammer Verlag published the final version of the Sternheim manuscript in October 1969. The book – now entitled *Carl Sternheim: Kritiker und Opfer der Wilhelminischen Ära* (*Carl Sternheim: Critic and Victim of the Wilhelmine Era*) – caused considerable uproar amongst literary circles due to its confrontational stance against Sternheim and its highly polemical nature. The densely-written study received a considerable number of reviews in various journals and newspapers, including a fervent riposte in the major national paper *Die Zeit*, in which a particularly enraged reviewer claimed:

> Everything that Sebald writes is sheer nonsense.... Once you have read the book through, you have the feeling that Sternheim is not

the critic and sacrificial victim of the Wilhelmine era but the sacrificial victim of the critic W.G. Sebald, a trainee grammar-school teacher. (*SM* 86)

Carl Sternheim, in many respects, was a minor target. Today, he is all but forgotten. At the time, however, the German-Jewish playwright enjoyed a massive comeback on the German post-war stage, mainly due to the patronage of Wilhelm Emrich. A widely respected *Germanist*, Emrich was the epitome of the older generation of professors Sebald despised for their lack of opposition to fascism. His resentment was not misplaced at all. Originally a member of the communist student organization, Emrich joined the Nazi Party in 1935 and served it dutifully in various high-ranking positions, including a stint at Goebbels' Ministry of Propaganda. After the war, Emrich blossomed into a fervent democrat, enabling him to pursue a distinguished academic career that culminated in a chair at the Free University Berlin – not an unusual German career trajectory at the time.

As the truth about Emrich's complicity was only publicly revealed in 1996, two years before his death, Sebald could not have known how spot-on he was in two respects. Firstly, his blanket distrust of the leading figures of German Studies (as well as other disciplines) was only too justified. Secondly, he had correctly detected the ploy prevalent among the ranks of the old guard of *Germanistik*, namely to embrace Jewish writers – despite evident literary deficiencies in some cases – to cover up their former fascist leanings.

In addition to Alfred Döblin, who was the subject of Sebald's controversial PhD thesis, the list of names in this category of Jewish writers shrewdly fêted by the German critical establishment includes the Polish-born concentration camp survivor Jurek Becker and the German writer Alfred Andersch, both of whom became the subjects of Sebald's scrutiny in the 1990s. In each case Sebald paired criticisms of the quality of their work with displeasure over the inability of his peers to identify them. Not surprisingly, these highly polemic attacks initially provoked a massive backlash from *Germanistik* as being widely off the mark. And indeed, Sebald always employed highly problematic critical tactics to argue his contentious opinions. *Inter alia*, Sebald takes quotes out of context, makes indefensible generalizations, issues one apodictic statement after another, ignores contradictory evidence or oversteps certain limits, particularly when he describes Sternheim and Döblin as inadvertent pioneers of Nazi ideology. Sober literary criticism this ain't. Yet in each case Sebald makes valid points and offers a new, provocative (or rather, thought-provoking) perspective. In the case of Andersch, Sebald's attack even led to a much-revised assessment of this former figurehead of German post-war literature over the last few years.

The Sternheim book – Sebald's controversial entry into academic publishing – is also marked by a characteristic common to his subsequent critical writings, namely a hidden and indirect autobiographical quality. Sebald's main argument about Sternheim's malaise can be summarized thus: as a Jew living in the chauvinistic and anti-Semitic society of imperial Germany, Sternheim had to betray his Jewish origins by adopting the prevalent social norms in order to win over the literary world. This kind of forced assimilation inevitably created an aggressive streak that Sternheim channelled into his satirical plays of social criticism; poking fun at the petty bourgeoisie, he hoped to gain not just recognition as an artist but also admission into the higher social circles of staunchly chauvinist Wilhelmine Germany. Caught in a web of unresolvable contradictions, Sternheim's literary work is beset by troubling political and ethical questions. This, for Sebald, is also confirmed by the fact that he eventually suffered a mental breakdown – therefore making Sternheim both a critic *and* a victim of his society.

But now consider the angry young academic Sebald studying Sternheim in various foreign countries during the late 1960s, a time when many of his generation were taking to the streets. Taking issue with the academic establishment in the realm of literary criticism is most certainly a contribution to the student protests at a distance. At the same time, this academic guerrilla warfare was also a reflection of Sebald's troubled relationship with his father and the entire generation of passive Nazi collaborators he represented in the mind of his son. Most crucially, Sebald's attempts to assimilate into the socially privileged realm of academia mirrored Sternheim's contradictory position. Not only was he hampered by his provincial origins, Sebald was also repelled by an academic discipline dominated by professors he mostly despised. Unlike Sternheim, though, he refused to make the necessary concessions to be accepted into the fold, but rather went abroad to operate like a partisan on the margins of *Germanistik*.

*

In this peripheral position, Sebald could only rely on himself. He did not reap the benefits of class privileges or influential mentors who could have helped him carve out a career. In December 1968, he applied for a prestigious Junior Research Fellowship at Sidney Sussex College, Cambridge to undertake doctoral research on Alfred Döblin. To this end, he asked his intellectual father figure from Frankfurt to act as a referee, but Adorno was too busy to reply to the letter from England. It made little difference, one can assume, as the élite institution would probably have rejected Sebald anyway.

In autumn 1969, Sebald returned once again to Manchester to embark on his doctoral thesis. At the newly established University of East Anglia, founded in 1963, his application for a position as Assistant Lecturer proved successful, and he began his appointment in October 1970. At least for the time being, Sebald had found his ideal academic home: the School of European Studies consisted mostly of young, enthusiastic staff and, as his long-time colleague Richard Sheppard affirms, 'the interchange between people working across a range of languages and disciplines – unusual in British universities at the time – made for a very creative atmosphere' (*SM* 88). Similarly, the pastoral charm and 'olde worlde' feel of East Anglia appealed to Sebald, as did the medieval town of Norwich, which at the time was still a secluded idyll largely untouched by the impact of modernity.

He vigorously pursued his research on Döblin. As usual, Sebald largely ignored academic conventions and norms when it came to writing his thesis. Later he would describe his approach to research thus: 'You find odd details which lead you somewhere else, and so it's a form of unsystematic searching, which of course for an academic is far from orthodoxy, because we are meant to do things systematically' (*EM* 94). Needless to say, he employed the very same method when writing his imaginative prose later.

Despite this inability to follow the rules, Sebald did nevertheless manage to complete his thesis within the required three-year period. Titled *The Revival of Myth: A Study of Alfred Döblin's Novels* and comprising some 300 pages, the manuscript was submitted in August 1973.[9] Like his book on Sternheim, the polemical tone and Sebald's quirky methodology caused his examiners to voice concern about the unorthodox nature of the thesis. However, they were ultimately swayed by the evident passion that the candidate demonstrated in making his case. As in his thesis on Sternheim, Sebald focused on a German-Jewish writer who was persecuted by the Nazis. Again, Sebald argued that – with the exception of the renowned novel *Berlin Alexanderplatz* (1929) – Döblin's entire *œuvre* was deficient and that *Germanistik* at large had failed to recognize this. Just as in his earlier Sternheim book, Sebald clearly aimed to reverse the received perception of Döblin – from Nazi victim to Nazi facilitator. Why condemn Döblin so harshly? There are a number of explanations, including Döblin's conversion to Catholicism in 1941. (To Sebald, this was tantamount to political treason given its timing shortly before the pinnacle of the Holocaust.) More importantly, Sebald was strongly repulsed by the many detailed scenes of torture, mutilations, killings, mass murder and all other sorts of barbaric acts in which people were brutally murdered in Döblin's work. While he acknowledged that *Wallenstein* (1920) or *Berge, Meere, Giganten* (1924–32) were intended to shock the reader into a rejection of violence, in Sebald's view, their principal effect was first to dull the moral sensitivity of the reader and then to exert an irrational fascination for violence. This allure, Sebald strongly believed, paved the way for the very real violence that the Nazis would soon put into practice.

In Sebald's view, Döblin's failure as a writer was therefore both artistic and ethical as he, albeit inadvertently, encouraged a revival of atavistic, barbaric notions termed as 'myth' by Sebald. The lesson to be extracted from Döblin, for Sebald, was incorporated into his own writing: never to evoke acts of cruelty directly – particularly as regards the Holocaust – but rather in a tangential way: 'I would never attempt to describe a scene of violence in a realistic fashion. The only way to write about persecution and its consequences is to approach the subject obliquely' (*CB* 146).

In July 1974 Sebald was awarded his doctorate. However, it took him until 1980 before he found a publisher for his thesis. He tirelessly approached one after another and tried to use his contacts – all to no avail. When the book finally appeared under the title *Der Mythus der Zerstörung im Werk Döblins* (*The Myth of Destruction in Döblin's Work*) in a revised German version, it essentially disappeared without a trace. Unlike the stir caused by the Sternheim book a decade earlier, this time no one was really interested in what Sebald had to say about the author except within a small circle of Döblin specialists. Probably due to this lack of wider recognition, Sebald lost interest in Döblin. In June 1983 he gave a provocative paper during a Döblin conference at his *alma mater* Freiburg where he denounced the writer as a proto-fascist, homosexual, and necrophiliac. Obviously, all these claims were unfounded and actually libellous. The audience, which included Döblin's son in the front row, was outraged, and rightly so. Sensing this hostile reaction, Sebald left the room immediately after he had finished his paper. And he never returned again to Döblin.

*

In June 1976 Sebald bought the Old Rectory in Poringland, a village some six miles south of Norwich. The building was dilapidated and urgently required renovation. With due attention to detail, the nineteenth-century charm of the house was

Illustration 3: Old Rectory in Poringland, Norfolk

17

tastefully restored and served as Sebald's home until his death. He much preferred his small upstairs study in the Old Rectory to his office in the modernist Arts Block of his university. Both his critical essays and his later literary texts would be written in this retreat, which also featured a picturesque garden, making it a quintessential English home for a German expat with a longing for times gone by.

During the 1970s, Sebald wrote a series of essays on major Austrian authors with whom he felt a particular affinity. Apart from Frank Kafka, his literary guiding star, these included Peter Handke, Thomas Bernhard, and the later Nobel laureate Elias Canetti. Sebald had met the latter by chance on a flight from Zurich to London, and struck up a conversation with him, eventually becoming a visitor to Canetti's Hampstead home. The schizophrenic poet and long term psychiatric patient Ernst Herbeck, on whose poems Sebald published a ground-breaking essay in 1980, was also a personal acquaintance. In *Vertigo*, Sebald describes a day trip he undertook with Herbeck, who had written poetry of breath-taking beauty and vulnerability. He felt a particularly close bond to this social outsider whose writings were completely ignored by mainstream German Studies. The insightful essay on Herbeck was therefore primarily intended as both an act of rehabilitation and a gesture of solidarity. Sebald also wrote a touching piece on Herbeck which appeared in a national newspaper in December 1992, more than a year after the death of the admired poet (*CS* 125–33).

From the early 1990s, Sebald's critical focus shifted from Austrian to German literature. What had vexed him from early in his life was not just the tacit silence about the violence of National Socialism but also the profound taboo on discussions of the Allied air war. In 1982 Sebald published *Zwischen Geschichte und Naturgeschichte: Versuch über die literarische Beschreibung totaler Zerstörung* (*Between History and Natural History: On the Literary Description of Total Destruction* (*CS* 65–95). This seminal essay already contains the major ideas that would be explored in more detail in the later Zurich lectures he gave on air war and literature in late 1997. These lectures proved highly controversial in Germany and, in 1999, they were published in a volume entitled *Luftkrieg und Literatur* (*On the Natural History of Destruction*).[10] In both his early essay and the later book, Sebald

18

strongly criticized 'the inability of a whole generation of German authors to describe what they had seen, and to convey it to our minds' (*NHD* x). After the war many writers had to hide their moral shortcomings and complicity with the Nazi regime. To convey the truth, in Sebald's mind however, is the prime duty of literature:

> The works produced by German authors after the war are often marked by a half-consciousness or false consciousness designed to consolidate the extremely precarious position of those writers in a society that was morally almost entirely discredited. To the overwhelming majority of the writers who stayed on in Germany under the Third Reich, the redefinition of their idea of themselves after 1945 was a more urgent business than the depiction of the real conditions surrounding them. (*NHD* ix)

Therefore, in Sebald's opinion, post-war literature contributed to the overall conspiracy of silence rather than destroying it. The only exception for Sebald are those authors who use a more documentary approach – Hans Erich Nossack, for instance, but particularly Alexander Kluge. His autobiographical and semi-documentary text-image collage *Der Luftangriff auf Halberstadt am 8. April 1945* (*The Air Raid on Halberstadt on 8 April 1945*) served as a very important inspiration for Sebald's own literary texts.

At the outset of the 1980s, Sebald planned to write a collection of essays aimed at correcting the established view of post-war German literature. As his unpublished notes indicate, his book would have highlighted the failure of renowned authors to convey an authentic portrayal of life under the Nazi regime against insights provided in books by writers who originated, as he once put it, 'from the other side'. That is to say, Jewish and Communist authors who had first-hand experience of persecution and were therefore able to tell stories and talk about experiences that people in post-war Germany did not really want to hear. Indicative of this comparative approach was an essay that appeared in 1983, entitled *Konstruktionen der Trauer: Günter Grass und Wolfgang Hildesheimer* (*Constructs of Mourning: GG & WH* (*CS* 97–123)). Following an introduction in which Sebald expounds the main deficit of post-war literature, namely its 'inability to mourn' (Alexander Mitscherlich), the essay contrasts Hildesheimer's haunting novel *Tynset* (1965) with Grass's hybrid text *Diary of a Snail* (1972). According to Sebald, Hildesheimer, who had escaped the Nazi death machine by emigrating to England, manages to convey a sense of melancholy about the atrocities of the Holocaust without alluding to it in any way. (Note the clear similarities to Sebald's later fictions!) Grass, on the other hand, portrays himself as the epitome of the morally and politically upright German, strongly criticizing his compatriots for hiding far too many skeletons in their closet. While Sebald agrees with Grass's diagnosis about the habit of refusing to admit to one's failings and to mourn the victims of the atrocities committed by the German nation, he questions the authenticity of his melancholy. Once again, Sebald's prescience regarding manoeuvres to hide an unsavoury past was confirmed when, in 2006, Grass revealed his membership in the Waffen-SS as a 17-year-old soldier. He, who repeatedly reproached his compatriots for their unwillingness to face up to their crimes, and who portrayed himself as a sort of 'moral consciousness of the nation', had himself hidden the truth about his biography for many decades. (Grass, by the way, was not an isolated case; unwelcome revelations about other leading intellectual protagonists of the cultural scene of the Federal Republic also came to light during the 1990s.)

The envisaged essay collection on post-war literature was never completed as such. Sebald rather published its planned chapters as individual essays during the 1980s and up into the early 1990s. Also, instead of only dealing with the morally complacent German post-war authors he disliked, Sebald increasingly concerned himself with émigrés such as the German-Jewish writer and socialist Peter Weiss. He wrote a touching and insightful essay on him in 1985 in which he persuasively argued that the strain of working on his monumental four-volume antifascist novel *Die Ästhetik des Widerstands* (*The Aesthetics of Resistance*) in fact represented a form of self-annihilation for the deeply melancholic Weiss. Deviating from academic orthodoxy in a number of ways, the essay was an exercise in empathy with a fellow melancholic Sebald admired and with whom he strongly identified (*NHD* 169–99).

The same year, 1985, also saw the publication of *Die Beschreibung des Unglücks* (*The Description of Misfortune*), Sebald's first collection of essays on Austrian literature. It took him nearly seven years to interest a publisher in the volume, which was well-received when it eventually appeared. Among many remarkable pieces, it contains an essay on Adalbert Stifter, a figurehead of literary conservatism and nature writing. Undermining the dominant line of thinking, Sebald tried to prove that the compulsive eater Stifter actually entertained fetishist tendencies and was suffering from repressed pederastic desires. By honing in on the real (or alleged) ambivalences in Stifter's writing, Sebald tried to prove that he was a modern writer. His highly speculative reading, directly connecting biographical details to the literary text, unsurprisingly caused concern and protest amongst Stifter experts. His essay paints a pathographic portrait of the writer which constitutes less fact than fiction; in this sense, it paves the way for the appearance of authors like Kafka, Swinburne and Conrad as subjects of his forthcoming imaginative writings. Shockingly, a terminally ill Stifter ended his life by slitting his throat; a violent death that links him with another writer who would also take his own life: Jean Améry (né Hans Maier) was an Austrian Jew who fought against the Nazis but was captured and tortured in Breendonk, Belgium, as described in detail by Sebald in *Austerlitz*. Though he survived incarceration in various Nazi camps and later wrote stunningly perceptive essays on his experiences, Améry could never come to terms with his own survival against all odds and finally returned to Austria from his Belgium exile to commit suicide in a Salzburg hotel room. During the second part of the 1980s, Sebald wrote four essays on Améry and developed an interest in the disorder called 'survivor's syndrome'. First described by the psychoanalyst William Niederland, this tragic behavioural pattern causes survivors of persecution to commit suicide towards the ends of their lives. The syndrome provided the cue for the stories in *The Emigrants*, which deal with authentic cases of people such as Sebald's former primary school teacher in Sonthofen and an ex-landlord in Norfolk, who had been damaged by anti-Semitism and committed suicide at a late stage in their lives.

Sebald's decision to take up literary writing himself in the 1980s was motivated by a number of reasons that are difficult to disentangle retrospectively. As he explained:

> I never had any ambitions of becoming or being a writer. But what I felt towards the middle point of my life was that I was being hemmed in increasingly by the demands of various things that one has in one's life, and that I needed some way out. (*EM* 98)

One aspect was Sebald's dissatisfaction with the majority of German post-war literature; frustrated by the dearth of literary texts he actually considered relevant and meaningful, he began writing literature himself:

> Most of the literary texts that had been written in Germany in the 1950s and 1960s about the Fascist years were dismal failures, marked largely by tactlessness and by very dubious moral positions, particularly as regards the representation of Jewish lives. So I felt it was necessary to at least attempt to write about these lives in a different sort of way. (*CB* 161)

This, of course, Sebald managed to do in a most astonishing manner which, according to some fervent critics, would elevate him to the status of redeemer of the German-Jewish cultural symbiosis.

The next aspect to consider is Sebald's unhappiness with the rules and strictures of academic writing. As mentioned before, already as a graduate student he was unwilling to adhere to the norms of professional discourse, from the artificial way in which one is supposed to discuss texts objectively to the tedious necessity of furnishing his essays with references.

> I was always intent on developing hypothetical notions to suggest that there is circumstantial evidence for a certain case. . . . I constantly came up against a borderline where I felt, well, if I could go a little further it might get very interesting, that is, if I were allowed to make things up. That temptation to work with very fragmentary pieces of evidence, to fill in the gaps and blank spaces and create out of this a meaning which is greater than which you can prove, led me to work in a way which wasn't determined by any discipline. (*CB* 151–2)

Kafka is the paradigmatic interface for this birth of literature from the spirit of academic writing. While Sebald's first two articles on *The Castle* from the early 1970s are still fairly orthodox, his essay published in 1986 takes some of Kafka's stories as the departure point for a speculative meditation about mankind's evolution gone astray. With *Dr K. Takes the Waters at Riva*, the third story in *Vertigo*, Sebald then fully crossed the vital borderline that separates critical from imaginative writing.

Thirdly, and arguably most importantly, it was the increasing loss of academic freedom caused by the burgeoning bureaucratization of higher education in Britain that led him to search for intellectual and artistic refuge. Sebald denounced the restructurings that were introduced under Thatcher in the 1980s as 'Stalinist', explaining in a 1998 interview with *The Observer* that the 'conditions in British universities were absolutely ideal in the Sixties and Seventies. Then the so-called reforms began and life became extremely unpleasant'.[11] Sebald felt such anger over the deterioration of academic freedom that he equated it to an attack on the quality of his life, which forced him to seek out a way to protect himself: 'One of the best means of self-defence, as one knows, is to go into the potting shed and build something that no one understands or no one knows what it is meant to be. This is how the writing of literary texts began for me' (*CB* 152).

Sebald's prose-poetry triptych *After Nature*, the first part of which appeared in a literary magazine in 1984, is commonly held to be his initial stab at imaginative writing. Little known, however, is the somewhat surprising fact that his first serious literary attempts were film scripts. No later than 1981, he drafted a script for German television on the life and death of the philosopher Immanuel Kant. Despite initial assurances that it would be produced for the small screen, this never happened. Sebald then tried to place it with radio stations and some theatres but to no avail. It remains unpublished for the time being.[12] In the same way, Sebald's more experimental *Leben Ws: Skizze einer möglichen Szenenreihe für einen nichtrealisierten Film* (*The Life of W: Sketch for a Possible Scenario for an Unrealized Film*) on the philosopher Ludwig Wittgenstein was written in 1986 but failed to materialize as a film production. It was, however, published in a German national newspaper in 1989 (*SM* 324–33). Intriguingly, an unsuccessful grant application held in his personal archive proves that as early as 1987 Sebald had already drafted the ideas for the stories that would form the core of both *Vertigo* and *The Emigrants*. The initial reactions of German critics and readers to his books *After Nature* (1988) and *Vertigo* (1990)[13] were mostly positive though limited to a small circle of literary aficionados. The fact that Sebald was extremely reluctant to engage in any kind of self-promotion (with the exception of the odd interview he granted to journalists visiting him in Norwich) did not help to increase his profile in the German literary scene.

However, *The Emigrants* (1992) was discussed in a popular

23

literary TV programme and this secured Sebald a good deal of publicity in Germany alongside many favourable reviews. Based on this success, *The Rings of Saturn* (1995) was also well-received. And yet, despite these achievements, Sebald suffered a crisis when tackling his next book project. As its working title suggests, *Aufzeichnungen aus Korsika. Zur Natur- & Menschenkunde (Notes from Corsica. On Natural History & Anthropology)*, was based on notes and observations that Sebald had made during two visits to the French island. He was particularly fascinated by both the archaic customs that had survived on Corsica and the island's largely untouched nature. Napoleon too presumably played a crucial role as Sebald perceived the French *empereur* as a sort of precursor to the dictators of the twentieth century. We can only speculate why Sebald never completed the book. He probably feared that it would have been too close to *The Rings of Saturn* in terms of structure and themes. Or maybe he realized that the concept he had originally envisaged would take too long to be turned into a book. After all, as he once explained at a public appearance: 'It's not like being a solicitor or a surgeon, you know: if you have taken out 125 appendixes, then the 126th one you can do in your sleep. With writing, it's the other way round' (*EM* 112). Some parts of the draft versions that survived the several *auto-da-fés* he undertook in the fireplace of his home were posthumously published in *Campo Santo*.[14] Undoubtedly the Corsica book, if finished, would have been another example of Sebald's remarkable gift for writing outstanding prose fiction. As a torso, it is a testament to his often crippling distrust in the actual quality of his writing.

In order to find a way out of the crisis which abandoning the Corsica project had caused, Sebald turned to critical writing. *Logis in einem Landhaus (A Place in the Country, 1998)* is his third collection of critical essays. It deals with writers from the Alemannic region, which comprises south-western Germany and the German-speaking parts of Switzerland – writers with whom Sebald felt deep empathy such as Johann Peter Hebel, Gottfried Keller and Robert Walser. As he uncannily states in the foreword, his essays aim to 'pay my respects to them before, perhaps, it may be too late' (*PC* 1). Upon closer inspection, however, one has to conclude that Sebald is actually writing about himself. The essays, superbly translated by Jo Catling, are as much autobiography as an homage to congenial colleagues. Highly poetic and critically instructive, these texts constitute quite a unique way of writing about literature. From the second half of the 1990s, 'the essayist can no longer be distinguished from the writer' (CS ix), as Sven Meyer rightly stated. Not only did Sebald dispense with the ballast of scholarly references, he now also inserted illustrations into the essays just as in his literary texts. And it is for this reason that *A Place in the Country* may rank with his imaginative books.

*

It was while Sebald was struggling with the ill-fated Corsica project that his fortune changed quite drastically. The English translation of *The Emigrants* had appeared in May 1996 and was soon met with rapturous praise from Susan Sontag in a short yet glowing review that set the tone for the enthusiastic response with which this and the following books by Sebald would be met: '*The Emigrants* is the most extraordinary, thrilling new book I've read this year... indeed for several years. It is like nothing I've read this year, indeed for several years. It is an unclassifiable book, at once autobiography and fiction and historical chronicle. ... I know of few books written in our time but this is one which attains the sublime.'[15] With his third book, Sebald made a stunning entry into the Anglophone literary world. Sales on both sides of the Atlantic were staggering. Much to his own astonishment, within a few months more copies of the translation of his third book had sold than of all German originals combined.

The question of how to disentangle the author Sebald from the narrator of his fictional texts is a tricky one. Most autobiographical elements of the 1990s related by the narrator are authentic though never fully accurate. For instance, the story of Henry Selwyn in *The Emigrants* is a truthful account of the events unfolding when Sebald and his wife moved into the home of the eccentric doctor – save for the relationship which connects him in the book to the deceased mountain guide Naegeli. Likewise, Sebald's hospital stay in August 1993 mentioned in *The Rings of Saturn* did indeed happen, as did the near-simultaneous deaths of his colleagues Janine Dakyns and Michael Parkinson in 1994.

The same applies to the problems with eyesight mentioned in *Austerlitz*; even the London doctor treating the narrator, as Sina Rahmani discovered, is genuine and his real name only slightly concealed. Sebald observed his own slowly deteriorating health from the mid 1990s on and attributed it to the demands his literary fame increasingly made on his body. He had to attend meetings with his publishers in Germany, the United Kingdom, and the United States. In addition, he undertook long book tours, and granted interviews and endured formal award ceremonies where, forced to don a suit and tie, he felt most uncomfortable – as several photographs taken at such occasions clearly show. Without doubt, fame came at a price. While Sebald was also busy overseeing the English versions of *The Rings of Saturn* and *Vertigo*, his work on *A Place in the Country* as well as the Zurich lectures on air war and literature had only provided temporary relief from the pressure to produce his next book of fiction. He was now well-known in literary circles in the Anglophone world, and had also gained deserved recognition. His admittance to the distinguished German Academy for Language and Literature in October 1997 was a significant acknowledgement of his achievements.[16] A few months later, he signed a contract with the renowned Wylie Agency in New York to represent him; another indication of his growing literary reputation in the Anglophone world.

*

All this took place, as we need to remind ourselves, against the backdrop of a full-time academic career that had become even more strenuous during the 1990s. The founding of the British Centre for Literary Translation (BCLT) in late 1989 is a case in point for the extra work Sebald put into his academic job, on top of regular teaching and administrative duties. The BCLT was an idealistic enterprise, an attempt to accord more recognition to the undervalued profession of literary translation as well as a contribution to cultural exchange between an often isolationist Britain and the rest of the world. Setting up the centre involved numerous trips to London to obtain funding for bursaries and staff, not to mention endless meetings with university officials who needed to be convinced of the inherent value of such a decidedly unprofitable enterprise. After the centre was success-fully established, Sebald's role was to ensure its financial stability – something that would prove to be a constant struggle and meant endless fishing for external funding. A new MA programme in Literary Translation was introduced in 1993 while conferences, special events, and an annual lecture series all had to be organized. The final battle Sebald fought against the bureaucratic behemoth was the introduction of an innovative PhD in Literary Translation. The programme would have made the BCLT financially viable through income generated by the fees. However, this plan was met with opposition by university executives and when Sebald came to the end of his five-year stint as director, he made no more efforts to fight against the drive to limit any potential expansion of the centre.

During the same period, the university management gradually reduced the languages offered at the School of Modern Languages and European Studies from the original six to just French and German. In 1998, the School was eventually restructured and renamed the School of Language, Linguistics and Translation Studies. Along with three other colleagues specializing in literature, Sebald was transferred to the School of English and American Studies. By now recognized as an accomplished writer, he was asked to deliver classes in creative writing. He did so, but with reservations, as he felt that writing was not necessarily a skill that could be taught because, not being a native speaker, he was worried about having to correct the students' English texts.

Sebald's increasing disillusionment with his situation at the University of East Anglia is ironically reflected in the comprehensive and semi-official *History of the University of East Anglia, Norwich* which contains no mention of him at all.[17] (One could guess though how the university would have claimed Sebald as an asset if he had indeed lived to win the Nobel Prize for which he was a serious contender.) The NESTA grant that Sebald was awarded in 2000 provided a very welcome liberation from academic duties as it would have reduced his workload to part-time status for the remaining years before his planned early retirement. And indeed, Sebald had started work on a new project, the exact details of which however will remain unclear until the ban on that material, which is stored in Sebald's literary estate at the German Literary Archive in Marbach, is lifted. From what is known about the 'World War Project', we have to assume that it would have been a kind of parallel examination of how people in rural France and rural Germany (possibly rural England, too) experienced the historical upheavals of the first half of the twentieth century. It is certain that Sebald's own family history would have played a central role in the book. Apparently, he aimed to trace his heritage back to the eighteenth century with a view to reconstructing how people on the margins both experienced and contributed to the destructive forces of history in the twentieth century. Questioned in 2001 on how he, as a German national, viewed his involvement in the fateful course of modern German history, Sebald explained:

> Although I was born 'late' and consequently was spared direct responsibility, I naturally feel at the same time that this is where my origins lie. My parents were involved in it and my grandparents' lives led up to it. The mistakes go a long, long way back. (CB 145)

The 'World War Project', one must speculate, would have attempted a kind of archaeology of his own existence, while also trying to situate his genealogy within the European dimension of the natural history of destruction.[18] And while we can assume that it would have been composed of elegant prose aiming to create a sense of levitation for the reader, the strenuous work required to bring it to life would have been anything but easy. According to Sebald in 2001:

> People who tend to have rather blithe views of life often consider that writing is a form of self-therapy. I don't particularly think so. Rather, I believe the more you turn your head towards things the more difficult it gets. From book to book it gets harder to look at determinants of your life again. ... These things, once you have seen them, have a habit of returning, and they want attention. I don't think that writing helps to exorcise the ghosts. (CB 145–6)

*

When the German version of *Austerlitz* appeared in February 2001, Sebald only had about ten months of life left. As previously mentioned, having delivered the kind of book that the literary market had expected of him, he had to fulfil numerous promotional obligations in Germany, the UK and the US. This became particularly intense when the English translation appeared in October of the same year. Short periods exempted, Sebald was constantly on the move and under pressure to make difficult decisions. At the very height of his fame, he was at the same time caught up in a tragic irony. Viewing academia as a dead end, he managed to extricate himself by writing literature only to discover that he had ended up in another trap. There would be no easy return to the undisturbed peace in the potting shed he enjoyed before his rise to literary prominence.

Talking to friends in the last few weeks before he died, he displayed a sense of exhaustion and even premonition of death. Yet he also had spells during which he evidently enjoyed the immense success he so rightly deserved. In mid November, he gave the opening speech for the *Literaturhaus* in Stuttgart, his final public appearance. At this occasion, he appeared comfortable and relaxed, and there is no indication whatsoever of what would happen one month later: on 14 December, while driving on a road near Norwich, he suffered an aneurysm and lost control of the car, veering directly into the path of an oncoming lorry. Winfried Georg Sebald, called Max by his friends and family, was buried on 3 January 2002 in a private ceremony at the nearby St Andrew's cemetery, Framingham Earl.

Illustration 4: Sebald in Stuttgart, 2001

2

After Nature **(1988)**

'In the future
death lies at our feet',
one of those obscure oracular sayings
one never again forgets.

(Sebald, After Nature)

It all started with a coincidence: on a train journey to London in the early 1980s, Sebald read a small book by the Austrian experimental writer Konrad Bayer. *Der Kopf des Vitus Bering* (*The Head of VB*) is a surrealist collage about the life and death of the seventeenth-century navigator who embarked upon his 1740 Arctic expedition accompanied by the German naturalist Georg Wilhelm Steller (1709–46). Sebald was struck by the fact that he shared his initials with the largely forgotten botanist and zoologist born in a place 'which my mother visited when she was pregnant in 1943'. The web of coincidences piqued his curiosity and the 'preoccupation with making something out of nothing, which is, after all, what writing is about, took me at that point' (*EM* 99).

Shortly thereafter, Sebald, who had been writing occasional poems of increasing length since the 1960s, began to compose a narrative prose poem about Steller's life, adventures and death. He investigated the fascinating story of the naturalist's emigration to Russia, his journey, with Bering, to the 'outermost sea', his years as a scientific hermit amongst the Koryak people and his solitary death from exposure. The resulting text consisted of twenty-one brief passages laying out fragmented episodes from Steller's biography – a literary portrait, blending fact and fiction, that ultimately tells us more about the author than the ostensible subject. Sebald characterized his motive for engaging with Steller as the 'temptation to work with very fragmentary pieces of evidence, to fill in the gaps and blank spaces and create out of this a meaning which is greater than that which you can prove' (*CB* 152). Sebald submitted *And if I remained by the Outermost Sea* to the Austrian literary journal *Manuskripte*, where it duly appeared in October of 1984.[1]

Another poetical prose-portrait followed suit, dealing with the mysterious figure of Matthis Grünewald: an eight-part meditation on the life and work of the reclusive German painter and the troubled times in which he lived. Though regarded as one of the foremost German Renaissance artists, alongside Albrecht Dürer and Lucas Cranach, Grünewald's identity remains strongly contested. Given the little that is known about the master artist, his biography, even more than Steller's life, provided a largely blank canvas where Sebald could fill in the gaps as he saw fit. His Grünewald is conceived as a melancholic mirror image of the author: a portrait of the artist as a pensive outsider at odds with the currents of his time. Once again, Sebald sent the text to *Manuskripte*, where it would appear with the title *As the Snow on the Alps* in June 1986.

In March 1987, a third, openly autobiographical prose poem appeared in the same journal. For *Dark Night Sallies Forth*, Sebald cannibalized a number of his unpublished poems to compose a fragmented account of his trajectory from rural Germany to provincial England. This self-portrait rounds out the previous two narratives, forming a trilogy that is ultimately about pilgrimages in search of wisdom, insight and truth. By arranging the pieces in chronological order under the title *After Nature*, the academic Sebald, aged forty-one at the time, commenced his first venture into the realm of literature.

After Nature was no mere overture: Sebald the writer had emerged fully-formed. Though initially little noted in Germany,[2] this epic poem showcased many of his greatest assets: his facility in fusing genres, in the reconstruction of biographies, his thematization of exile and melancholia, and his acute attention to paintings and images. As with *Vertigo* and *The Emigrants*, *After Nature* arranges disparate episodes into a formal unity best regarded as a literary triptych. In the German original, the long free-verse poem – a single entity in three parts – was subtitled *Ein Elementargedicht* (*An Elementary Poem*). Sebald, as Rüdiger

Görner argues, 'regarded his poem both as a statement on the basic elements (of culture) and an elementary attempt at continuing the epic tradition'.[3] The subtitle is, of course, as deliberately ambiguous as the title, which can be interpreted in three ways, all of which have a bearing on *After Nature*: first, as a reference to art as the faithful reproduction of a living subject – a matter of deep importance both to Grünewald and Steller; second, as an allusion to a mode of life dominated by technology, divorced from the natural world, and perhaps even to the apocalyptic time that succeeds the destruction of our natural environment; third, as a 'literal' translation of the Greek expression *meta-physics*, 'something that's always interested me, in the sense that one wants to speculate about these areas that are beyond one's ken, as it were' (*EM* 115).

The three sections of Sebald's debut cover about half a millennium, from the sixteenth-century to the present. They should primarily be read as a self-portrait in triplicate of their author: Grünewald represents Sebald the artist, similarly obsessed with suffering and pain; Steller stands for Sebald the academic, voluntarily displaced from his homeland; and the autobiographical narrator in the final section should be seen as Sebald's private side, an exploration of his roots as a child born in the penultimate year of the war and a recollection of his life as an emigrant in England. There are gaps not only in each of these three stories that aim to engage the reader's attention but also considerable differences between the three historical periods evoked. What connects the disparate circumstances related in the epic poem – the religiously determined medieval *Weltanschauung* of Grünewald, the pre-enlightenment coexistence of strict science and metaphysical speculation as encapsulated by Steller, and the technologically dominated modernity experienced by the narrator in the concluding 'pseudo-biographical' section (*EM* 168) – is man's increasingly troubled relationship with nature. As Sebald explained:

> It is a characteristic of our species, in evolutionary terms, that we are a species in despair because we have created an environment for us which isn't what it should be. We are living exactly on the borderline between the natural world from which we are being driven out, or we're driving ourselves out, and that other world which is generated by our brain cells. And so clearly that fault line runs right through our

physical and emotional makeup. And probably where those tectonic plates rub against each other is where the sources of pain are. (*EM* 56)

After Nature accordingly traces this very fault line in the minds and lives of the three protagonists. In a sense, the dominant perspective, which places man over nature, is being reversed in favour of an 'eco-centric' view, that is to say a holistic perspective which entails a concept of human history rooted in the framework of natural history. *After Nature* also makes a case for thinking in connective processes that not only permit a comprehension of the organic relations between man and nature, but also encourage the reader to look out for the subtle associations that bind the three sections. The most obvious examples would be the recurrence of the date of 18 May (on which Sebald was born in 1944) in two sections or the pivotal role of Windsheim, a provincial town in Franconia where the three lives examined in the poem intersect across time.

After Nature appeared during the heyday of the German green movement, which would profoundly change the political landscape in the wake of the 1986 Chernobyl disaster. Sebald certainly shared the sense of doom, feeling that because of 'our insane presence/on the surface of the earth' the ecological demise of our planet seemed inevitable, not least because creation develops as a 'regeneration proceeding / in downward orbits' (*AN* 26). His literary debut, however, does not subscribe to the view of nature prevalent at the time amongst ecologists or the emerging Green Party. Rather, Sebald followed the gnostic outlook pervasive in the early work of Thomas Bernhard, a writer he greatly admired: similar to the manic painter Strauch in Bernhard's debut *Frost* (1963), the mournful Grünewald sees human existence as preyed upon by bodily decay, constantly threatened by illness, and prostrate before horror and pain.

Close attention to these creaturely aspects of the human condition is a hallmark of Sebald's writing in general.[4] In *After Nature*, its emblem is the

> panic-stricken
> kink in the neck to be seen
> in all of Grünewald's subjects,
> exposing the throat and often turning
> the face towards a blinding light

(*AN* 27)

Grünewald painted these tortured creatures on his altarpiece at Isenheim, depicting the sick who sought succour for their ailments. For the narrator this agonized wrenching of the neck signifies

> the extreme response of our bodies
> to the absence of balance in nature
> which blindly makes one experiment after another
> and like a senseless botcher
> undo the thing it has only just achieved.
> To try out how far it can go
> is the sole aim of this sprouting,
> perpetuation and proliferation
> inside us also and through us and through
> the machines sprung from our heads

(AN 27)

The gnostic theme of a vicious inner impulse fuelling the destructive vector of natural history and thereby determining human existence finds its most extreme expression, according to Sebald, in Grünewald's Basel *Crucifixion* of 1505. In this extraordinary image, the 'landscape reaches so far into the depths / that our eyes cannot see the limits' while the scene on Mount Gethsemane is governed by a 'catastrophic incursion / darkness, the last trace of light / flickering from beyond, after nature' (AN 29f). Grünewald, the narrator speculates, may have been influenced by the eclipse of the sun of 1502, the 'event of the century, / awaited with great terror' at which he

> will have become a witness to
> the secret sickening away of the world,
> in which a phantasmal encroachment of dusk
> in the midst of daytime like a fainting fit
> poured through the vaults of sky

(AN 30)

No less than an anticipation of the apocalypse, the spectacle of the eclipse enabled Grünewald to cast 'a pathetic gaze / into the future' and to paint 'a planet utterly strange':

> Here in an evil state of erosion
> and desolation the heritage of the ruining
> of life that in the end will consume
> even the very stones has been depicted.

(AN 31)

So this is how it all ends: in the ultimate triumph of entropy, not only will all organic life perish, but even mineral formations will be annihilated. Whether Grünewald actually intended to convey such an impression through his painting is far from certain. But that does not detract from the vision conjured up by Sebald in his compelling account of Grünewald's work.

*

Although Georg Wilhelm Steller had 'abandoned / theology for the natural sciences' (*AN* 44), he initially retains a pantheistic view of the world. When confronted with the intimation that 'life diminishes, / everything declines, / the proliferation / of kinds is a mere / illusion, and no one / knows to what end', he responds with an evocation of 'the light of nature' (*AN* 50). The vestige of optimism thereby represented fades away as he witnesses the supremacy of hostile nature during his ill-fated expedition with Vitus Bering:

> For almost a quarter of a year
> the ship was tossed hither and
> thither, by hurricanes of a force
> none in the team could recall
> ever having experienced ...
> All was greyness, without direction,
> with no above or below, nature
> in a process of dissolution, in a state
> of pure dementia.
>
> (*AN* 63)

Soon the bodies of the crew are affected as well. Following the outbreak of scurvy, the 'sailors rotted away, till at last / there was scarcely a difference between / the living and the dead' (*AN* 64). Bering is no exception: with 'his face yellow-wrinkled, his mouth / toothless, a black ruin, plagued with boils and / lice all over his body' (*AN* 66) he provides a haunting spectacle of the creaturely duress of our presence on earth.

The lesson is clear: those who dare to map and conquer the unexplored corners of world are being taught a lesson for their hubris. The expedition, which required more than a decade of preparation, is also a poignant precursor of the megalomania characteristic of those contemporary undertakings whose inevitable failure is inscribed beforehand in the hypertrophic nature of their ambitions. Miraculously, Steller survives. Deciding not to return to civilization after his 'landfall / in the bay of Avatsha, he set out on foot for the peninsula's interior' (*AN* 70) to devote himself fully to his scientific pursuits:

> Steller collects botanical specimens,
> fills little bags with dried seed,
> describes, classifies, draws,
> sits in his black travelling tent,
> happy for the first time in his life.

(AN 72)

More conspicuously than elsewhere in *After Nature*, the Steller section offers an ambivalent portrayal of nature, contrasting its adverse features with the opportunity it provides to seek sanctuary from civilization. But Steller's serenity among the Koryak tribe is only temporary. Because he defends their indigenous rights against the Russian crown, the authorities prosecute him. In this way 'Steller now wholly grasps the difference / between nature and society' (*AN* 73).

Nature, Steller discovers, has ceased to provide a real safe-haven from modern civilization. What remains are

> Manuscripts written at the end of his life,
> ... an endless inventory,
> his zoological masterpiece,
> *De Bestiis Marinis*,
> travel chart for hunters,
> blueprint for the counting of pelts

(AN 74)

Sebald's true subject here is the advent of instrumental reason: what was originally conceived out of respect and deference to the magnitude and diversity of creation is distorted into a guide for the profit-oriented exploitation of nature and its resources. A particularly disheartening example is Steller's sea cow (*Hydrodamalis gigas*). The large marine mammal, first described by Steller in 1741, was hunted to extinction within twenty-seven years of its discovery.

The scientific exploration of nature leads to its colonization and plunder. Collective historical processes prove more powerful than individual intentions. And worse, in Sebald's eyes, human evolution and history are governed by a calamitous predisposition that outweighs all resistance and allows for no remedy: an overmastering destructive tendency, 'that cannot be / righted, too diffuse are / the workings of power, the one thing always / the other's beginning / and vice versa' (*AN* 102–3). It is this negative philosophy of history – gradually and unsystematically developed in his essayistic writings of the 1980s and then in his literary works of the following decade – that Sebald would eventually denominate the 'natural history of destruction'.

*

What Sebald attempts in the final section is a case study that situates himself as the subject of investigation. Here he aims to unravel entrapment of the individual in a web of contingencies that render useless the idea of self-determination. 'The illusion that I had some control over my life goes up to about my thirty-fifth birthday and then stopped' (*EM* 117), he confessed in an interview. Sebald's biography offers clear coordinates, yet the final section should not be taken at face value, especially as, even more than in the preceding sections, he performs here as an intra- and intertextual *bricoleur*. Apart from pillaging a considerable amount of text from his unpublished poetry, he used many quotes from numerous sources as diverse as the verses of Hölderlin, Albrecht von Haller and Paul Fleming, as well as the Bible, *King Lear*, and Disraeli, weaving them, mostly without acknowledgement, into his poem. The 'I' of the narrator is hence a product not only of its surroundings, but also of features drawn from other texts.

Making reference to astrology, the narrator classifies himself as a melancholic, thus providing a link with the protagonists of the previous sections. His ill-starred birth is recounted such:

> At the moment of Ascension Day
> of the year forty-four when I was born
> the procession for the blessing of the fields
> was just passing our house ... Mother
> at first took this as a happy sign, unaware
> that the cold planet Saturn ruled this hour's
> constellation and that above the mountains
> already the storm was hanging, which soon thereafter
> dispersed the supplicants and killed
> one of the canopy bearers.

(*AN* 86)

This ominous incident constitutes less an episode from the Wertach village history than a legend. The misfortune suggests the birth of someone whose life is marked by catastrophe, and indeed the narrator attests to the shadow cast over his life, saying 'I grew up, / despite the dreadful course / of events elsewhere... without any / idea of destruction' (*AN* 86–7). That is to say: despite obvious innocence about the crimes committed by his compatriots during the last year of Nazi rule, a moral guilt is accepted that would eventually lead Sebald to protest against the conspiracy of silence of the post-war years by scrutinizing the fate of victims of fascist prosecution.

The narrator goes further, implicating himself in the disastrous course of German history, claiming a kind of transgenerational traumatization: his pregnant mother, as we learn, witnessed the bombing of Nuremberg from a safe distance in late August 1943: 'She saw Nürnberg in flames, / but cannot recall now / what the burning town looked like / or what her feelings were / at this sight' (*AN* 84). This experience, the text implies, must have been passed along to her embryo. For when the narrator encounters by chance Albrecht Altdorfer's painting *Lot and his daughters* (1537), he suffers a disturbing return of the catastrophic *Urszene* as a *mémoire involontaire* (foreshadowing comparable flash-backs undergone by the protagonist of his later novel *Austerlitz*):

> On the horizon
> a terrible conflagration blazes,
> devouring a large city.
> Smoke ascends form the site,
> the flames rise to the sky and
> in the blood-red reflection
> one sees the blackened façades of houses.
> ...When for the first time I saw
> this picture in the year before last,
> I had the strange feeling
> of having seen all of it
> before, and a little later
> I nearly went out of my mind.

(*AN* 84–5)

It is here that the air raids against Germany come to the fore for the first time in Sebald's literary *œuvre*, revealing the extent to which this matter (in Germany long fraught with taboo and revisionist tendencies) occupied him, as yet another manifestation of the natural history of destruction in the twentieth century.

The narrator also finds ample evidence for the devastating *telos* of history after moving to Manchester in the 1960s. The decayed industrial metropolis, that 'the statesman / Disraeli (had) called / the most wonderful city of modern times' (*AN* 95), is a potent allegory for Walter Benjamin's insight that disaster and destruction are the insignias of the civilizing process. Desolate present and glorious past, industry and nature, reality and myth intertwine in Sebald's depiction of Manchester, composing an allegorical vision of a necropolis overhung with

> cotton clouds, those white ones
> into which without a word the breath
> of legions of human beings had been absorbed
> ... part of the obscure crowds
> who fuelled the progress of history.
> From my workplace I thought
> I could see the will-o'-the wisps
> of their souls, as with tiny lanterns
> they haunted the rubbish dumps
> of the City Corporation, a smouldering
> alpine range which, it seemed to me,
> extended into the beyond.
>
> (*AN* 96–7)

Anticipating the more detailed depiction of the city as being 'inhabited by millions of souls, dead and alive' (*E* 150) in the Max Ferber chapter of *The Emigrants*, the smoking chimneys of the incinerators conjure up the vision of crematorium chimneys. Metonymically, industry is linked with the Holocaust; factory *and* death factory reveal themselves as part of one continuum.

Tracing Sebald's trajectory, *After Nature* moves from industrial Manchester to rural East Anglia. Antedating, in many respects, the portrayal of Suffolk and its environs in *The Rings of Saturn*, the narrator takes his daughter on an excursion into the East Anglian countryside. Nature at first sight appears peaceful and untouched, dotted with historical monuments like the Anglo-Saxon grave at Sutton Hoo. But the longer they dwell there, the more the evidence of modernity's colonization becomes

Illustration 5: Manchester chimneys, photographed by Sebald

evident: 'now and then, / an old people's home, / a prison or an asylum, / an institution for juvenile delinquents' and in the distance lies 'the power station / at Sizewell, where slowly / the core of the metal / is destroyed' (*AN* 108). Steller's dilemma again: there is no longer any such thing as untainted nature; instead of peace and salvation the attentive observer cannot escape the melancholic realization that even in rural Suffolk surges the spectral presence of the untold number of victims of our aberration from nature, the collective cul-de-sac we are supposed to call progress:

> Tell me, child,
> is your heart as heavy as
> mine is, year after year
> a pebble bank raised
> by the waves of the sea
> all the way to the North,
> every stone a dead soul
> and this sky so grey?
> So unremittingly grey
> and so low, as no sky
> I have seen before.

(*AN* 107–8)

What this reveals is a sense of intensified *Heimatlosigkeit*, the utter absence of any place one can call home. No wonder then, that the concluding part of *After Nature* is devoted to an escapist fantasy: in a dream of flying (incidentally a recurrent motif in Sebald's texts), the narrator undertakes an imagined journey to Munich to see Altdorfer's painting *The Battle of Alexander at Issus* (1529). In accordance with the ecstatic nature of the journey, the impressive depiction of combat, as re-imagined by the painter, appears like a vision in front of the narrator, who in his turn attempts to visualize it for the reader in a powerful *ekphrasis*.

First, he looks at the human cost: 'Far more than one hundred thousand, / so the inscriptions proclaim, / number the dead over whom / the battle surges for the salvation / of the Occident' (*AN* 111). In contrast to the plethora of soldiers dead and alive, we find, at 'the centre of this grandiose thronging . . . , / Alexander, the Western world's hero' (*AN* 111). The reader should be cautious, though, of Sebald's ironic insinuation: Alexander the Great is not only a hero; for Sebald, his exploits as a world conqueror also made him the model for the imperialist fantasies of later military commanders such as Napoleon or Hitler.

What really attracts the attention of the observer-narrator is the grandiose depiction of nature by Altdorfer, an immense vista with an apocalyptic storm looming in the background. From his elevated perspective, 'as with a crane's eye', he surveys 'the incomprehensible / beauty of nature that vaults over' the battle scene and allows us 'to see that side of life that / one could not see before' (*AN* 112). What is revealed here through an unbounded, painterly gaze is an opportunity to look into the cosmic dimension of creation – a metaphysical opening into a timeless realm after nature.

3

Vertigo (1990)

> It was an eccentric pastime that no one knew about
> ... I just pottered away and produced these bits.
>
> (Sebald in Conversation with Chris Bigsby)

When *Vertigo* was published in 1990, two of the four separate yet interlocking narratives that constitute Sebald's first book of prose had already appeared, as in the previous case of *After Nature*, in the magazine *Manuskripte*. In an interview in 1992 he revealed:

> *Vertigo* came about by chance. I bought Stendhal's *De l'amour* in a bookshop in Lausanne. It resonated with a great many things that were on my mind because it contained many Italian place names which were familiar to me from the trips I'd made to Italy as a child. I knew Kafka's works well, but not Stendhal's, and yet I was immediately struck by a remarkable convergence. Stendhal was born in 1783, Kafka in 1883. Stendhal stayed in northern Italy in 1813, Kafka in 1913. So then I wrote two literary-biographical essays on the two authors whom I wanted to bring closer together. While I was doing that writing, I remembered that I, too, had travelled through northern Italy in 1980. I wrote an account of that trip in the long story *All'estero*, which ended up as a part of a triptych in between the stories about Stendhal and Kafka. That is how the book structured itself. In the fourth and final part, *Il ritorno in patria*, I recalled my childhood in the little village of Wertach. It is an attempt on my part to shed light on an emotional propensity of which I became extremely conscious for the first time when I experienced it in the late 1970s: the crisis that besets you in midlife. I wanted to know where it came from. I wrote the final part as a search for my own 'I'. (*SM* 350)

Again, a chance discovery, an alertness for coincidences and a feeling that one's own life is inexplicably entangled with those before us led Sebald to engage with the biographies of other writers. Abandoning both verse and fragmentation, Sebald now wrote prose proper; a truly remarkable prose that retained its lyrical denseness and prosodic quality yet made no attempt to sound 'contemporary' in any way. The texts on Stendhal and Kafka blurred the borderline between academic research and fiction, criticism and literature to create what Sebald tentatively described in the interview quoted above as 'literary-biographical essays'. Rich in intertextual references and allusions, all four stories reverberated with the tradition of European literature. Kafka's enigmatic fragment *The Hunter Gracchus* (1917) plays a key role as it assumes the function of a *Leitmotif* that skilfully connects the stories to create a disparate whole.

In this innovative prose work, Sebald employs the strategy which was to become his artistic signature for the first time – the inclusion of diverse visual material ranging from found objects (such as ticket stubs and newspaper clippings) to shrewdly manipulated photographs. While cleverly employed, this technique wasn't in fact Sebald's invention. Rather, he benefited from a broad tradition of text-image-montages in German literature, including the idiosyncratic books of the cultural critic Klaus Theweleit, the literary diaries of Rolf Dieter Brinkmann and the semi-documentary fiction of Alexander Kluge. With the downright manic emphasis placed on the coincidences encountered by the narrator during his Italian travels, as well as those resonating within and between the four different stories, Sebald manages to bring about what Eric Santner dubbed 'spectral materialism' – a phenomenon which can be only be grasped in special moments or places and implies an uncanny interference of past and present, absence and presence or the real and the mythical. This haunting feature manifests itself in an abundance of unlikely coincidences or odd recurrences throughout *Vertigo*.

Reading *Vertigo* relentlessly begs the question: could it really have been that way? In the same vein as in *After Nature*, the book requires, and rewards, disobedient and adventurous readers: readers who call into question the credibility of the narrator and who use the texts as a starting point for their own investigations into the dubious claims being made in the books. In this respect, Sebald may justifiably be called a postmodern writer. After all, he writes not to console or to entertain the reader but to challenge – and to sensitize. 'To read with vigilance is to question authority',[1] Sebald said in one of his last interviews.

*

The volume begins in the early nineteenth century: in the first story we learn of one Marie Henri Beyle, aged 17, participant in Napoleon's momentous crossing of the Alps in May 1800. Informed readers will realize that this person is none other than the writer also known as Stendhal, despite the fact that Sebald refers to him throughout by his real name. The march across the Great St Bernard Pass was a decisive event in military history. It is yet another example of those mammoth logistical enterprises prototypical of modernity. Accordingly, the narrator stresses the strongly asymmetrical relation between the powerful commander Napoleon and the amorphous, nameless mass of people under his authority.

Sebald viewed Napoleon's imperialist actions as the decisive factor in the misalignment of the course of European history in the nineteenth and twentieth century. As historians would agree, French occupation of Prussia and the German territories from 1804 inaugurated the Franco-German enmity which poisoned the relationship between these two nations at the heart of the continent until the second half of the twentieth century. Following the Franco-Prussian war of 1870–1, both World Wars can be placed in the framework of revenge taken for national humiliations suffered on both sides and at the hands of both nations. What was even more worrying, according to Sebald, was how the ruthless *Empereur*, Napoleon, set the model to conquer Europe by any means necessary and thereby, as Sebald strongly believed, paved the way for the mass-murdering *Führer* Hitler.

Beyle, or Love is a Madness Most Discreet provides a biographical sketch of Beyle/Stendhal that hardly mentions his writings. These, however, are constantly present through marked and unmarked quotations. Apart from Stendhal's autobiography *The Life of Henry Brulard* (1835–6, publ. 1890), Sebald used *De l'amour* (1822) and Stendhal's diaries as sources. The main purpose of the first episode though is to introduce the theme of memory, which is a major occupation in the writings of both Stendhal and Sebald.

In the Stendhal story, one clearly sees Sebald's dual approach to memory. As he later explores in the stories that make up *The Emigrants*, Stendhal demonstrates symptoms of uneven memory which are also prominent amongst victims of Nazi persecution: 'At times (Stendhal's) view of the past consists of nothing but grey patches, then at others images appear of such extraordinary clarity he feels he can scarce credit them' (*V* 5). Stendhal also reveals how authentic memory is distorted by false recollections through visual representations. We learn that, while browsing through his old papers, Stendhal discovered an engraving of the city of Ivrea and felt 'obliged to concede that his recollected picture of the town in the evening sun was nothing but a copy of that very engraving'. For this reason, Stendhal discourages us from visual reproductions 'since before very long they will displace our memories completely, indeed one might say that they destroy them' (*V* 8).

As implied by the title of the story, Sebald connects the discourse on memory with the theory of love as laid out in *De l'amour*. Relating Stendhal's unrequited love for Métilde Dembowski Viscontini, the reader learns that the unwanted suitor managed to obtain a plaster cast of her left hand. For Stendhal, this item serves as a true fetish: 'That hand now meant almost as much to him as Métilde herself could ever have done. In particular, the slight crookedness of the ring finger occasioned in him emotions of a vehemence he had not hitherto experienced' (*V* 21). The decision to integrate a picture of the artificial hand into the text has to be seen as a hint by Sebald. Just as this artificial limb serves as a 'prosthesis of memory' which for Stendhal is a substitute for the presence of the absent yet real person, literature always replaces the described object or reality by placing a linguistic representation in its stead. In literature, any endeavour to replicate reality 'after nature' is bound to fail. Literary authenticity, according to Sebald, can only be attained by deviating from naturalistic ways of narration. From *After Nature* to *Austerlitz*, his goal is always to create a poetic truth, to make visible the invisible, to allow the metaphysical to enter into the profane. A perfect example for this strategy is the narrator's claim that Stendhal, while at the port of Riva, had seen 'two boys sitting on the harbour wall playing dice' and 'an old boat, its mainmast fractured two-thirds

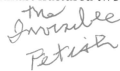
the Invisible Fetish

of the way up' from which 'two men in dark silver-buttoned tunics were at that moment carrying a bier ashore on which, under a large, frayed, flower-patterned silk cloth, lay what was evidently a human form' (*V* 25). A corpse, which the reader shall later learn is none other than the huntsman Gracchus.

*

All'estero (Italian for 'abroad') opens with a narrative entry typical for Sebald's prose texts:

> In October 1980 I travelled from England, where I had been living for nearly twenty-five years in a county which was almost always under grey skies, to Vienna, hoping that a change of place would help me get over a particularly difficult period in my life. (*V* 33)

Strolling aimlessly through the city, the increasingly exhausted narrator suffers from 'hallucinations' and imagines seeing people from his childhood village who 'had long since departed'. These uncanny apparitions induce a sense of 'a vague apprehension, which manifested itself as a feeling of vertigo' (*V* 35). Attentive readers will recognize it as the same sensation that took hold of Stendhal when he revisited the battle field of Marengo, realizing the stark difference between his vivid recollection of the skirmish that cost the lives of 16,000 men and the peaceful sight of the field some fifteen months later. Impacted by this confrontation with the traumatic memory, Stendhal is subject to 'a vertiginous sense of confusion such as he had never previously experienced' (*V* 17).

Vertigo, it is worth remembering, constitutes a disorienting phenomenon that affects both body and soul. The sensation is often accompanied by memory loss, a state of dizziness where the conventional logic of language and perception is eliminated. In the realm of art, vertigo corresponds to blurriness. In *Vertigo*, Sebald fittingly not only uses hazy photo material but also blurs the dividing line between the authentic and the fake. Everyday awareness of reality is undermined and destabilized. For example, in Venice the narrator encounters an English upper class tourist 'whom I immediately recognised as King Ludwig II of Bavaria' (*V* 53). Despite being fully aware that the tourist is not really identical with the deceased monarch, the narrator insists on him being a *doppelgänger* and *revenant* at the same time – identity oscillates, perception struggles in a grey zone of uncertainty.

Before the narrator sets off for Italy – which ever since Goethe's *Italian Journey* (1816) is considered the paradigmatic destination of German authors – he visits the schizophrenic poet Ernst Herbeck outside Vienna. Apart from introducing the central theme of madness, the episode in which the narrator relates his afternoon outing with Herbeck is also a touching memorial to an outsider, a writer whom Sebald admired and felt a very close kinship with. The empathetic literary portrait of Herbeck complements the ground-breaking essays that Sebald had devoted to his lyrical miniatures. At the same time, allusions to other German-language writers who ended in madness are evident in the short episode: one is reminded of Wilhelm Waiblinger's account of his visits to the famous eighteenth-century poet Friedrich Hölderlin, who was confined as a mad man in his tower on the Neckar river, as well as of Carl Seelig's book on his walks with Robert Walser, an inmate of the Herisau Asylum and the subject of a most touching poetical essay in Sebald's *A Place in the Country*. The headless portrait purporting to be of Herbeck is doctored, and it is in fact derived from a well-known image of Walser – yet another example of blurred identities.

All'estero abounds in such pairs, lookalikes, twins, *doppelgängers*, mirror images and other uncanny doublings. They are closely connected with the paranoid tendency of the narrator to uncover connections of all sorts between himself and the outside world, connections which he steadfastly believes to be meaningful signs. This narcissistic trait is being transferred to the reader, who is encouraged also to be on the lookout for hidden meanings and obscure analogies. Sebald's 'poetics of correspondence' is mirrored in the structure of the story, which relates two trips to major cities in northern Italy, with the second journey being a deliberate repetition of the first. The declared purpose of his second Italian journey is 'to probe my somewhat imprecise recollections of those fraught and hazardous days' (*V* 81).[2] Describing his first trip as 'hazardous' directs the reader's attention to the traveller's paranoid anxieties about the ominous 'Organizzazione Ludwig' threatening his life. This right-wing terrorist cell (consisting of only two men, as was later discovered) did truly exist; it killed fourteen people in northern Italy, and one person in Germany, between 1977 and 1984.

All'estero accordingly features a strange pair of young men, palpably following the narrator from Venice to Verona. Running scared, he seeks refuge in a *pizzeria*. While reading about the latest killing by the group in the newspaper, he also discovers that one Carlo Cadavero runs the restaurant. Overwhelmed by the accumulation of coincidences and implicit ciphers (authenticated by a reproduction of the restaurant bill), he decides to cancel his trip and immediately return to England. Seven years later, the second journey also proves overshadowed by menacing signs. The sight of a scared rat drowning in a canal makes the narrator leave Venice after only a few hours to continue his journey via Padua to Verona. Recalling that Franz Kafka spent an unhappy afternoon there, he decides to bypass the city and to continue, on the trail of Kafka's trip to Italy in September 1913, to Desenzano on Lake Garda.

References to Kafka feature heavily in the second part of *All'estero*. Arriving at Desenzano, the narrator visits the station's *pissoir*,

> where scarcely a thing had been altered since the turn of the century.... As I washed my hands, I looked in the mirror and wondered whether Dr. K., travelling from Verona, had also been in this station and found himself contemplating his face in this mirror. (*V* 86)

Yet another strange encounter that induces a feeling of vertigo in the narrator is experienced when he joins the bus to Riva: to his utter surprise

> a boy of about fifteen climbed aboard who bore the most uncanny resemblance imaginable to pictures of Franz Kafka as an adolescent schoolboy. And if that were not enough, he had a twin brother who, so far as I could tell in my perplexed state of mind, did not differ in the slightest. (*V* 88)

Double *doppelgängers* – indeed a bewildering incident to which Sebald adds a comic twist when the parents of the twins mistake the interest in their boys as the advances of a paedophile. As Sebald claimed at a public reading:

> That particular episode actually happened as it is described, and it was from that time onwards that I always have one of those small cameras in my pocket. (Audience laughter) It was a completely unnerving afternoon. It was really terrible. But, you know, it does happen. Doubles do exist. (*EM* 116–17)

But can we trust Sebald on the veracity of this grotesque episode? Does it, as ever so often, require our disobedience? Or is he rather playing a game with his audience here, similar to the deliberate confusion he creates around the autobiographical status of the narrator? Sebald evidently wants to keep us guessing. This can also be said of the episode set in Venice when the narrator meets a friend called Malachio. The question of whether the relationship between the two men may possibly be of a homosexual nature has occupied the minds of some scholars though the issue seems of little relevance here. What is more important is the fact that Sebald's type of narration in *Vertigo*, as Helen Finch showed, exhibits 'a radically queer textuality'.[3] The associative, oscillating, rhizomatic and paranoid text undermines the established generic norms of the crime novel, the *Bildungsroman*, travel writing and the historical novel. The fact that Sebald's male narrators often appear to be bachelors and that heterosexual encounters are virtually absent from his books offers hardly any material for gender theoretical speculations; it has more to do with his gnostic view of human reproduction as a way of prolonging the negative gradient of natural history's 'steeply descending downward slope'.[4]

Rather than to fall into the trap of speculating about the potential repressed sexual tendencies of Sebald or his private life as husband and father, we should devote more energy to considering the issue that Malachio brings up when he undertakes a boat trip with the narrator on the canals of Venice at midnight:

> Malachio told me that he had been giving a great deal of thought to the resurrection, and was pondering what the Book of Ezekiel could mean by saying that our bones and flesh would be carried into the domain of the prophet. He had no answers, but believed the questions were quite sufficient for him. (*V* 62)

During his second visit to Verona, the narrator by sheer coincidence (how else?) walks past the *pizzeria* of Carlo Cadavero, which he now finds boarded up. Enquiring about the reason of the closure at a near-by shop, his question is met with a 'screed of savage curses . . . which seemed directed less at myself than at some incident which had happened in the restaurant next door' (*V* 125).

One can therefore assume that this is a murder site, possibly by the Ludwig terrorist organization. At least this is strongly suggested because the unexpected confrontation with the place conjures up a 'dark apparition':

> The image that had lodged in my mind when I fled Verona... presented itself to me again, strangely distorted – two men in black silver-buttoned tunics, who were carrying out from a rear courtyard a bier on which lay, under a floral patterned drape, what was plainly the body of a human being. (*V* 125)

There he is again, the dead huntsman from Kafka's story, roaming this world because he is unable to find admission to the underworld, haunting not just the narrator but *Vertigo* itself with his ghostly presence in all four stories.

Visiting Milan Cathedral, the narrator suffers from 'recurring fits of vertigo' and is forced to acknowledge that the clarification he had hoped to achieve retracing his own footsteps through Italy still eludes him. On the contrary: 'Despite a great effort to account for the last few days..., I was unable to determine whether I was in the land of the living or already in another place' (*V* 115). In other words: like Gracchus, he finds himself once more in that borderline state which Sebald's books try to open up for the reader.

*

Dr. K Takes the Waters at Riva is quite an odd story. Not least because it most expressly demonstrates Sebald's transition from critical to imaginative writing. Kafka's *The Castle* was the topic of his very first academic article in 1972; in 1983, for the centenary, he produced a highly speculative essay on Kafka's evolution stories in English. Though commissioned by the *Times Higher Education Supplement*, the piece was never published there.[5] Next, he embarked on writing the story about Kafka, which made its first appearance in a small literary magazine called *proposition*, featuring images inserted into the text just as in the final, largely identical version contained in *Vertigo*. Kafka only left a few notes on his trip to Lake Garda in autumn 1913. Based on his sparse travel diary and letters to his fiancée Felice Bauer, Sebald undertakes a semi-fictional reconstruction of the trip, combining quotes, commentary and conjectures. Kafka spent three weeks, that much we know, at a sanatorium in Riva. While

attempting to gain some distance from the problematic relationship with Bauer, he begins a short-lived affair with a Swiss girl.
In the example of Kafka, as in the case of Stendhal (and
elsewhere), Sebald demonstrates that writers fully devoted to
their profession are unable to sustain a relationship. In early
1917, Kafka starts writing down the story of the hunter Gracchus
– one of very few texts that mention a real place name. The
narrator believes the autobiographical 'localization' to be
Kafka's way of coping with the experience of 'those autumn
days at Riva (which) had been so beautiful and so appalling' (*V*
163) at the same time.

For the third time, Sebald makes the mysterious trio appear in
the book, but finally the identity of the dead person is exposed:

> It is Gracchus the huntsman. His arrival was announced at midnight
> to Salvatore, the *podestà* of Riva, by a pigeon the size of a cockerel,
> which flew in at his bedroom window and then spoke into his ear.
> Tomorrow, the pigeon said, the dead hunter Gracchus will arrive. (*V*
> 164)

Finally, the previously inscrutable background story gets
revealed: Gracchus fell to his death while hunting a chamois
in the Black Forest. The narrator describes this incident as 'one
of the strangest items of misinformation in all the tales that have
ever been told' (*V* 165) since there are no such deer in that very
forest. Resembling the fate of the 'eternal Jew' dead Gracchus is
forced to roam the world of the living because 'a wrong turn of
the tiller, a moment of inattention on part of the helmsman'
meant that 'the barque which was to have ferried him to the
shore beyond failed to make the crossing' (*V* 165).

Sebald probably came across Kafka's enigmatic story in
Benjamin's seminal essay on Kafka, where Gracchus is understood to symbolize the Messiah. Sebald undertakes – just as in his
critical essays – a highly speculative biographical interpretation:
'It seems to me that the meaning of Gracchus the huntsman's
ceaseless journey lies in a penitence for a longing for love...
where there is seemingly, and in the natural and lawful order of
things nothing to be enjoyed' (*V* 165). That is to say, pointing to
the 'illicit emotion' that Kafka admits to in a letter to Felice,
namely that a man he vaguely knows suddenly became the
'object of fascinated interest in a way he cannot entirely explain

even to himself', prompting him to follow the man on the street and 'veritably lusting' with 'a feeling of unbounded pleasure' (*V* 166-7). Whereas Stendhal saw love as a form of madness, Kafka speaks of the 'terrors of love, which . . . stood foremost among all terrors of the world' (*V* 167). At least this is what the narrator claims to be Kafka's position. What constitutes poor scholarship makes for good literature, though: twisting quotes from Kafka's text and deliberately misconstruing Gracchus's gesture of placing his hand on the knee of Salvatore, the *podestà* (mayor) of Riva (whose name means 'redeemer'), Sebald arrives at 'a blatant act of misreading'[6] in his diagnosis of Kafka's repressed homosexuality. Conflating allegorical huntsman and real author, Sebald concludes his story with a rhetorical question that is ultimately directed at us, the readers:

> And how are we to fend off the fate of being unable to depart this life, lying before the *podestà*, confined to a bed in our sickness and, as Gracchus the huntsman does, touching, in a moment of distraction, the knee of the man who was to have been our salvation? (*V* 167)

*

Il ritorno in patria, Italian for 'the return home', is the title of the last story. The homecoming is not a nostalgic, but rather a truly elegiac affair involving a return to the repressed fears of childhood. Sad, disturbing memories, such as that of the burial of a one-week-old baby, are rekindled. There are likewise eccentric and despondent life stories, such as that of the melancholic village doctor who was destroyed by morphine, which are recounted to annihilate any impression of a rural idyll. Fatal accidents, severe illness and shattered hopes reveal themselves as the distinctive marks governing people's lives.

The narrative initially scandalized the inhabitants of Wertach because many felt that the village had been unfairly portrayed, particularly regarding its past. Even though it appears only as 'W.' in the fourth and final story of *Vertigo*, the biographical information on the book jacket stated the full name of Sebald's place of birth. These days, of course, Sebald is largely appropriated with pride in his village and the walk that is described at the beginning of the story is now designated the 'Sebald Trail' to attract tourists. The downward climb from the Oberjoch Pass to the village mimics a *katabasis*, a descent into the underworld – another recurrent trope in Sebald's works. It also carries echoes of Napoleon's crossing of the St Bernard Pass as well as the celebrated opening of Georg Büchner's prose fragment *Lenz*. The passage, where the narrator briefly pauses at the bridge, 'listening to the steady murmur of the river and looking into the blackness which enveloped everything' (*V* 183), recalls Kafka's land surveyor K., who similarly pauses at the bridge to listen to the river and stares into the darkness before entering the realm of the castle. At the Engelwirt (literally Angel Inn), where the narrator takes lodgings, he is allocated a room located at the very same spot 'where our living room had once been' (*V* 192), for when he was a child, his family used to live in a flat at that inn. While the thoroughly renovated rooms bear no trace of his former home, the uncanny return to the location evokes a vivid reappearance of childhood memories and creates an exemplary Sebaldian grey zone between past and present: 'The guest room... was a world away from (my childhood); I myself, though, was no more than a breath away, and if the living room clock had started chiming in my sleep, I would not have been in the least surprised' (*V* 195).

The huntsman Gracchus, too, makes his final, covert appearance in *Il ritorno in patria* via the mysterious 'grey chasseur' (*V* 222), allegedly residing in the attic of the Café Alpenrose. As the narrator recalls, the owners of this establishment used the 'grey hunter' as a bogeyman to prevent them as children from sneaking up into their attic. Now an adult, the narrator wants to finally solve the mystery and enters the attic with a former neighbour. There he discovers, amongst the chaotic assemblage of discarded and useless lumber untouched since his childhood days, 'something like an apparition, a uniformed figure' which turns out to be 'an old tailor's dummy, dressed in pike-grey breeches and a pike-grey jacket' (*V* 227). Yet even this disclosure does not destroy the power which this embodiment of childhood fears wields over him:

> Time and time again I dreamed, and still occasionally do, that this stranger reaches out his hand to me and I, in the teeth of my fear, venture ever closer to him, so close that, at last, I can touch him. And every time, I then see before me the fingers of my right hand, dusty and even blackened from that touch, like the token of some great woe that nothing in the world would put right. (*V* 228–9)

As it turns out, the uniform 'almost certainly belonged to one of the Austrian *chasseurs* who fought against the French irregulars', which links with the fact that a forbear of the café owners 'was killed in the terrible Battle of Marengo' (*V* 228). As attentive readers will recall from the first story, this is the very battle which Stendhal watched from afar and where, upon returning to the site, he suffered a bout of vertigo. Being confronted with the object of his childhood fears, the narrator remembers a vivid recurring dream in which the 'grey hunter' acts as an obvious harbinger of death. This leads him to relate the story of a severe childhood illness during which he felt death approaching. Due to his painfully slow recovery which lasted several weeks, the boy's return to health resembles a rebirth, as his revival symbolically coincides with the start of the new year.

The 'grey hunter' is also connected with the local huntsman Hans Schlag, who 'had managed extensive hunting grounds in the Black Forest for several years before moving from there to the district around W' (*V* 237). One day he dies – under suspicious circumstances, like Gracchus – by falling from a footbridge into a ravine. The child observes the return of his corpse to the village, on 'a woodcutter's sledge drawn by a heavy bay... upon it what was plainly the body of a man under a wine-coloured horse blanket' (*V* 246–7), and later learns 'that a sailing ship was tattooed on the left upper arm' (*V* 249) – the emblem of poor Gracchus.

Having spent a full month in W, the narrator decides to return to England. The long train journey to the port of Hook of Holland prompts the realization that not only his childhood village but also his fatherland has become foreign to him. 'Everything appeared to be appeased and numbed in some sinister way', he comments on the countryside, 'straightened out and tidied up as it is to the last square inch and corner' (*V* 253). Sebald grasps a welcome opportunity here to emphatically criticize contemporary Germany. Using well-known stereotypes of German order and tidiness, he criticizes the morally problematic tendency to tidy up the past. The landscape, the narrator complains, is 'thoroughly parcelled up and segmented', everything else is 'neatly delineated', even wheat 'emerges according to schedule', while there are 'ever-expanding colonies of family homes behind their rustic fences and privet hedges' and on 'the streets of the towns there were far more cars than people. It was as if mankind had already made way for another species, or had fallen under a kind of curfew' (*V* 253–4).

Back in chaotic London, the narrator visits the National Gallery before heading on foot to Liverpool Street station to catch his train home. Near the City, he passes a strange tube station entrance 'from which the familiar sweetish, dusty warmth of the subterranean world' (*V* 258) emanates. Once more, the realist story is undermined by Sebald: the narrator recognizes the station from previous tube journeys as that ghostly stop where 'no one ever embarked or alighted … and on not one occasion did any of the other passengers raise so much as an eyebrow' (*V* 259). The underground entrance reveals itself as a gate to the underworld, an opening to the realm of the dead – the traveller, however, refuses the opportunity to embark on the *katabasis* as he does 'not dare to take the final step' (*V* 259).

Recalling the poem *Day Return* (*ALW* 92–5), where the lyrical 'I' reads the description of the Great Fire of London in Samuel Pepys' diary while on a train from Liverpool Street station to Norwich, the narrator in *Vertigo* falls asleep and experiences a vivid dream. Walking through an arid, eerily lifeless desert, he stands on top of a cliff and notes 'a drop into truly vertiginous depths' and, on the horizon, he perceives a mountain range 'which I feared I would not be able to cross' (*V* 261–2). Truly, this has to be the land of the dead yet again. From this 'breathless void', the words, which he had previously read in Pepys' diary about the Great Fire, return as an apocalyptic vision of another city ablaze. Civilization is once more destroyed by fire. Progress, again, equated with destruction: 'And, the day after, a silent rain of ashes, westward, as far as Windsor Park' (*V* 263). With this sentence, adapted from Pepys, the English translation of *Vertigo* closes. It omits, however, something quite crucial from the German original: at the end appears the year 2013, followed by the word *Ende*.

This 'future' date, now already in the past, should not only be seen as a warning: it is critical to the summation of the historical lines linking the four texts. Apart from the biographical parallels between Stendhal in 1813 and Kafka in 1913, both years were historical turning points – Napoleon's demise followed by the inauguration of German nationalism via the Wars of Liberation in 1813, which later came into vile fruition in 1913 when Europe prepared for the Great War. '1913 was a peculiar year,' the narrator states, 'the times were changing, and the spark was racing along the fuse like an adder through the grass.... The sacred and righteous wrath of the nation was invoked' (*V* 121). And as we know now, that Great War only prepared for another World War, which will hardly be the last disaster in the natural history of destruction.

4

The Emigrants (1992)

> Sebald insisted, persuasively, that he was not interested in
> Judaism or in the Jewish people for their own sake. 'I have
> an interest in them not for philo-Semitic reasons', he told
> me, 'but because they are part of a social history that was
> obliterated in Germany and I wanted to know what
> happened'.
>
> (Artur Lubow: Crossing Boundaries)

The Emigrants transformed Sebald's literary fortunes – although
it certainly did not appear that way initially. When Sebald read
an excerpt from the book at the televised competition for the
Ingeborg Bachmann Prize in 1990, he did not convince the high-
profile judges. Scandalously, he failed to win any of the six
prizes handed out by the jury to emerging writers. Things
changed once the first enthusiastic reviews appeared in autumn
1992 and the book was featured on the popular TV programme
Das Literarische Quartett in January 1993.

Like *Vertigo*, the beginnings of the four stories collected in
this book hark back to the 1980s. The nucleus of *The Emigrants* is
the story of the damaged life and tragic death of Paul Bereyter,
the fictional name Sebald gave to his primary school teacher
Armin Müller. When Sebald heard the news of Müller's suicide
in early January 1984, it must have reminded him of Jean Améry,
another Jewish survivor of Nazi persecution who had committed suicide five years earlier. Sebald explained how a kind

> of constellation emerged about this business of surviving and about
> the great time lag between the infliction of injustice and when it
> finally overwhelms you. I began to understand vaguely what this
> was about, in the case of my schoolteacher. And that triggered all the
> other memories I had. (*EM* 70)

Researching and writing the story of his former teacher put Sebald on track of the phenomenon of the 'survivor syndrome'; a tragic condition that first causes its victims to repress their traumatic burden of escaping persecution before eventually becoming overwhelmed and compelled to end their lives. As before in *Vertigo*, Sebald collected four stories in one book, and, again, used the *Leitmotif* of a hunter to connect them – in this case the butterfly collector Vladimir Nabokov. One difference between the two, however, is that the coherence between the stories that make up *The Emigrants* is much stronger. Still, the title suggests a common denominator that does not really exist. Not only did two of the four titular migrants leave their home well before the persecution of Jews in Germany began after 1933, contrary to the blurb on the paperback editions of both the German and English editions, the book is certainly not about 'the lives of four Jewish émigrés in the twentieth century'.[1] After all, Ambros Adelwarth has no Jewish roots but had to leave for reasons to do with the economic situation in Germany, while Bereyter, according to Nazi racial arithmetic, was only a 'quarter Jew'.[2] But this lack of attention to detail is symptomatic of the widespread belief in Sebald's identity as a 'Holocaust author', a label he unreservedly rejected during the last few years of his life. Even though the genocide committed by the Nazis looms in the background in many of his literary writings, Sebald did not want to be classed together with authors who were either surviving victims of racial persecution or writers who aimed to exploit the Holocaust for sensationalist or provocative reasons to gain attention.

Sebald's literary project is thoroughly ethical. He traces the psychological after-effects of experiences such as expulsion, prosecution and dislocation. Tracing the four lives he reconstructs in his stories, he reflects on the suffering the victims of Nazi terror endured. He also aims to show that the loss of one's *Heimat* (a German word that means both home and homeland) as a result of forced migration is a paradigmatic experience of modern life. The victims of Nazi prosecution in this sense represent the most extreme instance of a destruction of traditional attachments to local and social ties (as Sebald's distant relatives had themselves experienced when they emigrated to the United Sates in the early twentieth century).

This process of erasing any traditional concepts of belonging – evidently a driving force of capitalism's push to 'globalize' the world – was for Sebald closely linked to both the destruction of traditional cultures and of the natural environment through industrialization.

A major factor for the success of the book was the seemingly authentic background of the four biographical stories – individuals with whom Sebald, thinly cloaked as the narrator, had come into contact either in person or through personal documents such as diaries, family photo albums, letters, and private papers. In accordance with ideas formulated by Walter Benjamin, the reconstruction of forgotten biographies is a kind of remembrance that seeks an active dialogue with the dead through a literary engagement with their life stories. Sebald's literary work aims at no less than a restitution of those who have been neglected by official historiography.

*

DR HENRY SELWYN

Sebald met the real life model of the protagonist of the first and shortest story when he moved to East Anglia in October 1970 and settled seven miles outside Norwich in the picturesque market town of Wymondham. To protect the identity of his former landlord, he changed the name to Henry Selwyn and used the name of a nearby village, Hingham. Nevertheless, nearly all the details of the narrative, including the personal traits of the characters that appear in it, are authentic.

When the narrator first meets the reclusive Selwyn, he assumes him to be leading an eccentric Englishman's life as 'a kind of ornamental hermit' (E 5) in a remote corner of the vast garden of a decaying property. But it emerges that Selwyn was born in 1892 in Lithuania and that he and his family were forced to flee in 1899 because of anti-Semitic pogroms. The Selwyns disembarked in London, wrongly assuming to have already reached their original goal, the United States. The protagonist tries to make the best of the situation; he studies and assimilates into British society, gets married and pursues a career as a medical doctor. Still, towards the end of his life, the past comes back to haunt him. Estranged from his dominant, business-minded wife, the evidently depressive Selwyn relates the details of his acquaintance with an older Swiss alpine guide he had met in the summer of 1913. As the narrator recounts, Selwyn confesses that 'never in his life, neither before nor later, did he feel as good as he did then, in the company of that man' (*E* 14).

Some critics tend to interpret this as homoerotic desire but the considerable age gap between the sixty-five-year-old guide and the young Henry Selwyn suggest that the nostalgic, wistful portrait of Naegeli is actually an homage to Sebald's grandfather. After all, Egelhofer was a close companion and experienced guide to his grandson during their long walks in the wilderness. Similarly, the news of Naegeli's death cast Selwyn 'into a deep depression. It was as if I was buried under snow and ice' (*E* 15). Selwyn appears to be not just deeply wounded by the insurmountable loss of his older friend, but equally troubled by disturbing memories of his expulsion from Lithuania. Long repressed, these memories return with an acutely destabilizing effect on his perception of self.

The news that Selwyn decided to take his life therefore doesn't come as much of a surprise to the narrator. Nevertheless, many questions linger. The reader is prevented from fully comprehending the motives for his suicide as crucial gaps and blank spots in the narrative are never revealed. This disturbing feature is amplified by the uncanny coincidence that many years after the suicide the narrator comes across a newspaper article reporting that 'the remains of the Bernese alpine guide Johannes Naegeli, missing since summer 1914, had been released by the Oberaar glacier, seventy-two years later. And so they are ever returning to us, the dead' (*E* 23). It is precisely this ghostly presence of the dead in the familiar realm of the living that underlies *The Emigrants*.

PAUL BEREYTER

The image at the outset of the second narrative shows railway lines in an open field from an unusual perspective. It soon becomes clear that this is the very perspective from which the primary school teacher Bereyter willingly awaited a gruesome death in the form of an oncoming train.[3] As the narrator explains, the cryptic remark in a local paper's obituary 'that during the Third Reich Paul Bereyter had been prevented from practising his chosen profession' (E 27) provoked his investigation. Sebald indeed researched the biography of his teacher Armin Müller, and incorporated some of his findings, such as photographs and newspaper cuttings, in the text. He also freely makes additions, such as ascribing to Bereyter characteristics taken from Ludwig Wittgenstein (who famously completed a spell of primary school teaching in Lower Austria).

Trauer um einen beliebten Mitbürger

Pädagoge Armin Müller erwarb sich große Verdienste um die Musik

SONTHOFEN th – Mit dem 73jährigen Armin Müller verstarb ein angesehener Bürger vor Sonthofen. Der geborene Immenstädter war ein beliebter Pädagoge und machte sich um die Musik verdient.

Seit Kriegsende übte er in Sonthofen seinen Lehrerberuf aus. Zehn Jahre war er ehrenamtlicher stellvertretender Schulrat neben seiner Tätigkeit als Klaßlehrer, die er bis zu seiner Pensionierung mit viel Geschick und Verantwortungsbewußtsein ausfüllte. Der musikbegeisterte Pädagoge und gute Pianist Armin Müller war auch auf musikalischem Sektor tätig. Die Stadtkapelle, damals Musikverein Sonthofen, unterstützte Armin Müller einige Jahre als Vorsitzender und Chronist. In der Anfangszeit der Jugendblaskapelle Sonthofen leistete er als Vorsitzender wertvolle Arbeit, ebenso als Bezirksleiter im Bezirk II Sonthofen des Allgäu-Schwäbischen Musikbundes. Der Jugendblaskapelle Sontho-

fen und dem Bezirk II gehörte er als Ehrenmitglied bzw. Ehrenvorsitzender an.

Beim Trauergottesdienst in der Friedhofskapelle betonte Dekan Ehle, aufgrund seines vorbildlichen Wesens und seiner Begabung, den jungen Menschen etwas beizubringen, von seinen Schülern immer geachtet und verehrt worden. Armin Müller habe als Mitglied, sowie der Schule immer vorbildlich und uneigennützig gedient, erklärte Rektor Adolf Lipp im Namen des Kollegiums der Grundschule Mitte. Für den bayerischen Lehrerinnen- und Lehrerverband, dem Armin Müller über 50 Jahre als Mitglied, Schriftführer und Vorstandsmitglied angehört hatte, nahm dessen Vorsitzender Hauser Abschied von dem Verstorbenen. Im Namen des Allgäu-Schwäbischen Musikbundes Bezirk II Sonthofen sagte Bezirksleiter Josef Eldracher Dank für all die Verdienste, die sich Armin Müller um die Musik erworben hat. Am offenen Grab nahm eine Gruppe der Jugendblaskapelle Sonthofen unter Leitung ihres Dirigenten Arthur Engeser musikalisch Abschied von ihrem Ehrenvorsitzenden und Träger der goldenen Ehrennadel, wobei Vorsitzender Manfred Schmid ein Gebinde niederlegte.

Nördlicher Landkreis
auf einen Blick

Illustration 6: Obituary of Armin Müller: 'The obituary in the local paper was headed "Grief at the Loss of a Popular Teacher" and there was no mention of the fact that Paul Bereyter had died of his own free will, or through a self-destructive compulsion.'

In this touching, semi-fictionalized memorial, Müller/Bereyter appears as the very opposite of the conservative, authoritarian type of teacher so prevalent in post-war Germany. He abhors 'Catholic sanctimoniousness' (*E* 35) and inspires his pupils by taking them for excursions to local workshops and factories. Crucially, Bereyter ditches the official textbook in favour of the *Rheinischer Hausfreund*, a collection of tales by Johann Peter Hebel (published 1807–34) that Sebald much admired.[4] Müller's unusual pedagogy, it can be argued, served as an early model for Sebald's own, often unorthodox, approach to teaching and the close relationships he formed with his students.

The most important source for the narrator's portrait of Bereyter is his long-time (and fictional) companion Lucy Landau. She relates many details revealing the depressive and suicidal disposition of Bereyter 'who was almost consumed by the loneliness within him' (*E* 44). Speaking to Landau, the narrator finally realizes the background of the remark in the obituary: the completion of Bereyter's teacher training almost coincided with the Nazi rise to power – just embarking on his career, Bereyter learns that having one Jewish grandparent made him unfit for his profession in the eyes of the Nazi state. 'For the first time', the narrator relates, 'he experienced that insuperable sense of defeat that was so often to beset him in later times and which, finally, he could not shake off' (*E* 49).

Sebald is always particularly interested in stories outside received narrative norms. Bereyter provides just that: unwelcome in his home country, he emigrates to France and works as a private tutor. The Nazi invasion then makes it unviable for him to stay on as a German, so he takes the desperate decision to return to his fatherland in 1939. There, in a darkly ironic twist, Bereyter soon gets drafted into the army and has to fight for six years in the war. He survives; though the reader does not learn any details, it appears that Bereyter is a truly damaged man. As an evident victim of a tragic double-bind, he gives in to homesickness and returns to the very place that that had initially ejected him, once more taking up his interrupted career as a teacher in rural Allgäu. Even though he later decides to leave Germany yet again, his previous two paradoxical homecomings are mirrored by his final journey to S(onthofen). Just like Améry, who travelled from Belgium to Salzburg to commit suicide in a hotel, Bereyter returns to the Allgäu to die on a railway track. This terrible death has a haunting hold over him: there 'could be little doubt that (his former love) Helen and her mother had been deported, in one of those special trains that left Vienna at dawn, probably to Theresienstadt in the first instance' (E 49–50). Clearly, the choice of death constitutes a sort of re-enactment of their fate, instigated by a deep sense of guilt of having being unable to save them, and fulfilling his uncle's prophetic comment that he would 'end up on the railways' (E 63) in a truly vertiginous way. Also, this suicide has to be understood within a wider context of a protest against the oblivion which characterizes the approach of the people of Sonthofen, as evidenced by the oblique remark in the obituary, which is authentic.[5] Fighting against their concerted will to deny the historical burden, and the collective responsibility for the crimes committed, Sebald's literary commemoration reconstructs those fates which the ruthless process of history aims to obliterate.

AMBROS ADELWARTH

With his third story, Sebald engages his own family history. What we learn about the emigration of his relatives to the United States in order to escape the economic hardships of Germany after the First World War, is, with minor exceptions, based on true facts. That also applies to the journey the narrator undertakes in the early 1980s in order to trace the peculiar life of his great uncle Ambros Adelwarth, who had emigrated before the Great War. As the narrator explains, he had seen his great uncle only once, at a family gathering in 1951, during one of his visits back home. He remembers Adelwarth as 'a most distinguished presence' (E 68) who easily out-classed his relatives, adding: 'I do recall being deeply impressed by the fact that his apparently effortless German was entirely free of any trace of our home dialect and that he used words and turns of phrase the meanings of which I could only guess at' (E 68). An advanced, sophisticated command of language here figures as a result of the decision to leave behind one's roots, and in this sense Adelwarth prefigures the development that characterizes

Sebald's own path from local dialect to world literature.

Working in various service positions, Adelwarth's trajectory took him to Montreux, London, Japan, Monte Carlo and other locations far from his Allgäu home. Eventually, he finds his lifetime post as 'major-domo and butler with the Solomons..., the wealthiest of the Jewish banking families in New York' (E 87–8). Especially close is his relationship with the family's son Cosmo, whom he serves as valet and who is also, as is clearly suggested, his sexual partner. Together, the pair traverse the world on journeys to far-away destinations such as Greece, Turkey, Egypt, and the Holy Land. But this luxurious, carefree lifestyle could never last very long: the atrocities of the Great War have a deleterious effect on Cosmo's mental health, for the 'more it raged, and the more we learnt of the extent of the devastation, the less Cosmo was able to regain a footing in the unchanged daily life of America' (E 95). In what could be described as psychotic episodes of pathological empathy, Cosmo seems to see 'the inferno, the dying, the rotting bodies lying in the sun in open fields. Once he even took to cudgelling the rats he saw running through the trenches' (E 95–6). His condition improves after 1918, though only temporarily. At the end, he is institutionalized in Ithaca, New York, only to '(fade) away' (E 98) soon after admission. A distraught Adelwarth, the narrator learns from his relations, returned to service at the Solomon residence for over two decades until his retirement.

Having lost his immediate purpose in life, the past comes back to haunt him as it does the other figures in the book. Mirroring his companion's fate, Adelwarth consigns himself to the very same sanatorium, and also perishes there. Retracing his footsteps some thirty years later, the narrator learns in 1984 of the brutal regimen undergone by the inmates of the asylum. The director of the clinic subscribed to treating his patients with 'what was known as the block method, a course of treatment... which not infrequently involved more than a hundred electric shocks at intervals of only a very few days' (E 112). As we realize, along with the narrator, both Cosmo and Ambros succumbed to a form of penal suffering that 'really came close to torture or martyrdom' (E 111).

A strange inversion: while the privileged banker's son Cosmo shares the misfortune of the soldiers of the First World War, his

German valet follows in the path of his Jewish lover. Two forms of redemptive suicide, harking back to the similarly motivated deaths of Selwyn and Bereyter. But in Sebald's literary universe, the dead never vanish for good. In September 1991, the narrator sees them in the French seaside resort of Deauville, where the pair had spent the summer of 1913,

> taking tea out in the courtyard, or in the hall leafing through the latest papers. They were silent, as the dead usually are when they appear in our dreams, and seemed somewhat downcast and dejected. Generally, in fact, they behaved as if their altered condition, so to speak, were a terrible family secret not to be revealed under any circumstances. (*E* 122–3)

Remembrance is the key for allowing the dead to maintain their ghostly presence in the realm of the living. The empathetic search for traces of his ancestors allows the narrator to enter the same liminal sphere that is also inhabited by Gracchus, grey zone between life and death, present and past, presence and absence.

The role of the uncanny huntsman linking the four lives in *Vertigo* is here taken up by the ominous 'butterfly man' who can often be seen outside the sanatorium in Ithaca, a 'middle-aged man holding a white net on a pole in front of him and occasionally taking curious jumps. Uncle Adelwarth... said: "It's the butterfly man, you know. He comes round here quite often" ' (*E* 104). He is none other than Nabokov (who indeed taught English literature at nearby Cornell University at the time), and who also appears in the Henry Selwyn story. There Sebald inserts a picture of Nabokov taken in 1971 into the text, showing the Russian émigré novelist with his butterfly net on a mountain near Gstaad. In the Paul Bereyter story, the teacher first approaches and speaks to his confidante Lucy Landau when he finds her on a park bench reading Nabokov's autobiography *Speak, Memory* – clearly linking the allegorical figure with the process of memory. And in the final story of *The Emigrants*, the butterfly man even makes two more appearances, confirming his status as the hidden link connecting the stories.

MAX FERBER

The fourth story is the most outstanding part of this remarkable book. As before in the concluding story of *Vertigo*, the narrative is markedly autobiographical, compellingly augmented by fictive elements. The Holocaust, so far only subtly present in the stories, now gains a more prominent thematic presence. Frank Auerbach is easily identified as the model for the painter Max Ferber,[6] although Sebald changed several aspects of his life such as locating his studio in Manchester rather than in the English capital. Another person who contributed to the figure of Ferber is Peter Jordan, Sebald's first landlord in Manchester. This crucial shift in Sebald's biography is described in the opening section of the narrative. Taking up the negative portrayal of a crumbling Manchester in *After Nature*, the narrator again talks about the bouts of depression that overcame him as a result of his perambulations through 'a soot-blackened city that was drifting steadily towards ruin' (E 176):

> I never ceased to be amazed by the completeness with which anthracite-coloured Manchester, the city from which industrialization had spread across the entire world, displayed the clearly chronic process of its impoverishment and degradation to anyone who cared to see. (E 156)

What is extraordinary is that Sebald metonymically connects the destruction wrought by industrialization with the Holocaust in a variety of mostly subtle ways. As he explained in an interview: 'The only way in which one can approach these things, in my view, is obliquely, tangentially, by reference rather than by direct confrontation' (*EM* 80). In the Ferber story, the chief vehicle is the symbol of the chimney, which connects the factories with the crematoria of the concentration camps. Manchester, once eulogized as 'the industrial Jerusalem' (E 165), figures in the story allegorically as a colossal 'death factory', being 'built of countless bricks and inhabited by millions of souls, dead and alive' (E 150).

The contentious nature of the fundamental correlation between technological progress and barbaric genocide is evident when the Jewish refugee Ferber explains to the narrator that when I arrived in Manchester I had come home, in a sense, and with every year I have spent since then in this birthplace of industrialization, amidst the black façades, I have realized more clearly than ever that I am here, as they used to say, to serve under the chimney. (*E* 192)

Ferber thereby illustrates that even though his exile in England saved his life, it was neither a true escape from the evils of the Holocaust, nor did it provide him with a new home. Rather, the city was more of a penance: 'Manchester has taken possession of me for good. I cannot leave, I do not want to leave, I must not' (*E* 169). Even more significant is the episode recounting the one and only time Ferber left Manchester in 1966 in order to visit the famous Isenheim Altarpiece painted by Grünewald: the forceful passages describing the entombment of Christ thematically connect *The Emigrants* with *After Nature*; and Ferber, too, feels spiritually akin to his painterly colleague Grünewald:

> The extreme vision of that strange man, which was lodged in every detail, distorted every limb, and infected the colours like an illness, was one I had always felt in tune with, and now I found my feeling confirmed by the direct encounter. The monstrosity of that suffering, which, emanating from the figures depicted, spread to cover the whole of Nature, only to flood back from the lifeless landscape to the humans marked by death, rose and ebbed within me like a tide. Looking at those gashed bodies, and at the witnesses of the execution, doubled up by grief like snapped reeds, I gradually understood that, beyond a certain point, pain blots out the one thing that is essential to its being experienced – consciousness – and so perhaps extinguishes itself; we know very little about this. (*E* 170)

What Ferber refers to in this visceral discussion of pain, agony and torture is the experience of physical violence he was spared because of his timely escape from persecution; while at the same time Grünewald's singular vision, in Ferber's *ekphrasis*, reverberates with the atrocities of the Holocaust.

Shortly after his trip to Colmar, Ferber travels on to Montreux where he climbs Mount Grammont. It is on the top of the mountain – which he had last visited with his father many decades ago – that the painter has his brush with the allegorical butterfly collector: a 'man of about sixty suddenly appeared before him – like someone who's popped out of the bloody ground. He was carrying a large white gauze butterfly net and said, in an English voice that was quite refined but quite unplaceable, that it was time to go down' (*E* 174). Yet another *katabasis*, it seems, which might explain why Ferber kept 'no recollection of the descent with the butterfly man (as it) had disappeared entirely from his memory'. In order to conquer the 'lagoon of oblivion (which) had spread in him' (*E* 174), Ferber works for almost a year on a portrait entitled *Man with a Butterfly Net*. But it is to no avail – the process of recollection fails, the portrait shows a faceless figure. The narrator provides a detailed description of the exhausting work and despair involved in painting what Ferber considered his 'most unsatisfactory work' (*E* 174), causing him sleepless nights due to his increasing agitation about the failure to complete it. Ferber's obsessive 'work at the easel ten hours a day' (*E* 177) appears as a kind of drudgery, a form of serfdom; a recurring motif in Sebald's literary as well as critical writings. One suspects this suggestion can be attributed to Sebald's own reconsideration of his texts in particular and writing in general, which he once described as 'embarking on the hopeless task of finding the truth'.[7] The special relationship between narrator and painter is not just apparent in their shared first name, Max, but also by the fact that Ferber entrusts to him the papers of his mother, Luisa Lanzberg. True to form, Sebald describes this inheritance as 'one of those evil German fairy tales in which, once you are under the spell, you have to carry on to the finish, till your heart breaks, with whatever work you have begun – in this case, the remembering, writing and reading' (*E* 193).

The memoirs are authentic; they originate from an aunt of Peter Jordan, Sebald's landlord in Manchester, who handed them over to his erstwhile tenant for creative use. The embedded narrative sticks closely to the memoirs, though Sebald adds hidden quotations from other sources and also makes some small yet significant alterations. One crucial addition is the episode in which young Luisa remembers a Russian boy, about ten years old, 'leaping about the meadows with his butterfly net; I saw him as a messenger of joy' as he opened 'his specimen box and released the most beautiful red admirals, peacock butterflies, brimstones and tortoiseshells to signal my final liberation' (*E* 214). It is the final time that the butterfly man materializes in the book; while the adolescent

Luisa believes him to be the harbinger of a better future, the reader knows that her hopes are all in vain. Working with this authentic material, albeit with poetic licence, Sebald takes up the role of a kind of ghost writer of the victim of the Holocaust. As her papers were written in 1939 to 1941, the impending annihilation is palpable for those who read the story; yet Luisa Lanzberg herself does not concern herself with her future, but only her past. Precisely because of its exclusion, the Holocaust attains an eerie, foreboding presence in the text. Lanzberg's recollections of her childhood and youth in rural Germany provide a paradigmatic case of how a fully assimilated middle-class family was slowly transformed into an object of racial persecution. Her story serves as an example for the cultural loss for German society caused by the extermination policy of the Nazis. Moreover, readers are given an opportunity to attempt the impossible: to imagine the magnitude of the loss inflicted upon the world by the Nazi death machine.

Learning about the fate of the Lanzbergs, the narrator embarks on a search for traces of their family history in contemporary Germany. Needless to say, this is not a straightforward search-and-rescue mission. The most telling example of the fraught nature of this project is the episode in which the narrator is forced to climb over the wall of the Jewish cemetery housing the remains of the Lanzberg family. Official policy, it would appear, is to bar access to the unseemly aspects of German history, provoking those interested in this narrative to perform acts of disobedience. Upon finding their gravestone, the narrator discovers that Ferber's extended family perished in the Holocaust, with one exception: 'Only Lily Lanzberg, who took her own life, lies in that grave. I stood before it for some time, not knowing what I should think; but before I left I placed a stone on the grave, according to custom' (E 225).

The story closes in a circular fashion, like so many of Sebald's stories, with the narrator's return to Manchester in order to visit Ferber, who has been hospitalized with a serious illness. Back in his hotel, he is reminded of a photo exhibition on the Litzmannstadt ghetto that the Nazis established in the Polish city of Łódź, 'once known as polski Manczester' (E 235). Sebald once more follows Adorno by establishing a causal connection between industrialization and extermination, progress and barbarism. The photos in this exhibition were taken by a Nazi official named Walter Genewein and remain conspicuously absent in *The Emigrants*, a book abounding with illustrations. One of them, however, is verbally evoked: it shows 'three young women, perhaps aged twenty' who sit behind the frame of a loom. But as the narrator maintains, it is not he who looks at the picture but rather, in a surprising twist, the women look at him, as it were, from *across* the photo: 'I cannot make out their eyes clearly, but I sense that all three of them are looking across at me, since I am standing on the very spot where Genewein stood with his camera' (E 237).

Illustration 7: Photograph taken by Walter Genewein of three women in the ghetto Litzmannstadt

Surprisingly, Sebald often proved unable to produce poignant conclusions to his stories. Take, for example, the banal closing sentence in *Austerlitz*, or the end of *All'estero*, where a postscript on Verdi is appended without really adding anything to the story. In contrast, *The Emigrants* closes with the narrator's striking contemplation of the photo. The accusing gaze of the women from beyond enables a shocking insight: the narrator cannot help but follow in the footsteps of the Nazi photographer and, in a way thus becomes one with the fascist perpetrator. To make matters worse, he suddenly recognizes the fabric woven by the three Jewish girls as resembling the fabric of 'the settee in our living room at home' (*E* 237).

Sebald once remarked in an interview that 'certain things emerge from images if you look at them for long enough' (*EM* 165). The photograph discussed here is a case in point. Firstly, the narrator realizes that the petty bourgeois household in the Allgäu is intricately linked with the foreign ghetto; there is no difference between the place of protection and belonging and the seemingly extraterritorial place of extermination abroad. Secondly, the narrator comprehends that there can be no innocent position when looking at pictures taken by Nazi perpetrators; again, a seemingly natural dividing line is dissolved. No surprise, therefore, that the narrator finds himself in a very troubled state, particularly as 'the woman on the right is looking at me with so steady and relentless a gaze that I cannot meet it for long' (*E* 237).

It is in this tension-laden condition that – in yet another twist – something utterly surprising occurs: the three nameless victims – who in all likelihood will have perished in the mass liquidation of Polish Jewry – transform from anonymous victims to mythological figures under the empathetic gaze of the narrator: 'I wonder what the three women's names were – Roza, Luisa and Lea, or Nona, Decuma and Morta, the daughters of night, with spindle, scissors and thread' (*E* 237). It is to such breath-taking transubstantiation that Sebald referred when he maintained that 'only in literature ... can there be an attempt at restitution over and above the mere recital of facts and over and above scholarship' (*CS* 215).

5

The Rings of Saturn **(1995)**

> Moving from one subject, from one theme, from one concern, to another always requires some sleight of hand.
>
> (Sebald on *The Rings of Saturn*)

The Rings of Saturn is Sebald's masterpiece and probably the most extraordinary book in recent German letters. It defies classification more than any other piece in Sebald's *œuvre*, as it freely crosses genres such as autobiography, biography, travelogue and meditative essay. With astounding ease, the narrative blurs the boundaries between fact and fiction, art and documentary – navigating a wide-ranging literary territory across the temporalities of past, present, future. In the German original, *The Rings of Saturn* was subtitled *Eine englische Wallfahrt* (*An English Pilgrimage*): an apt classification for the remarkable psycho-geographical journey that Sebald embarks on with his readers, traversing time and space in a search that strives less for truth than for redemption.

A melancholy perambulation across the Suffolk countryside provides the narrative framework of the book. At the outset, however, it is worth pointing out that this walk never took place as described. Rather, Sebald made various walks from summer 1992 to spring 1993 that were supposed to result in ten short essays to be published individually in a German newspaper. But as soon as he started composing the pieces, they grew into something more elaborate. More specifically, they transformed into a sophisticated reflection of Sebald's melancholic conception of a natural history of destruction: linking rural East Anglia with imperial China, the haul of herring with the Holocaust, or merging his own biography with those of other writers – Sebald uncovers hidden traces of destruction that add up to a universal history of catastrophe and reveal mankind as an aberrant species. The details related by the narrator in *The Rings of Saturn* largely correspond with actual facts: the narrator's time in the hospital, as well as the deaths of Sebald's colleagues Janine Dakyns and Michael Parkinson, are all true. The 'long stint of work' (*RS* 3) mentioned in the first sentence refers to *The Emigrants*. And the eccentric model maker Thomas Abrams – whose detailed model reconstruction of the Temple of Jerusalem built on a remote farm in the countryside sounds like a classic Sebaldian invention – did indeed exist.[1]

The title of the first version of the manuscript was *Unter dem Hundsstern* (*Under the Dog Star*), and indeed on the initial page Sebald refers to 'the old superstition that certain ailments of the spirit and of the body are particularly likely to beset us under the sign of the Dog Star' (*RS* 3). Nonetheless, the planet that turned out to be the book's lodestar is Saturn, the celestial body traditionally associated with melancholia. Accordingly, the musings on melancholia by the seventeenth-century philosopher Thomas Browne provide important reference points for Sebald.

The quirky polymath from Norwich appears as both predecessor and model for the narrator. Browne, he claims, insisted that 'all knowledge is enveloped in darkness. What we perceive are no more than isolated lights in the abyss of ignorance, in the shadow-filled edifice of the world. We study the order of things, says Browne, but we cannot grasp their innermost essence' (*RS* 19). Read in this context, Sebald's literary pursuits are marked by the desire to shed at least some light onto this darkness. And for all his resistance to academic conventions, Sebald deeply believed in the mission of the humanities (as of art) to be able to achieve this goal. The narrator's key assessment of the quality of Browne's writings can also be understood as a poetological statement by Sebald, who shares his passion for

> constructing labyrinthine sentences that sometimes extend over one or two pages, sentences that resemble processions or a funeral cortège in their sheer ceremonial lavishness. It is true that, because of the immense weight of the impediments he is carrying, Browne's writing can be held back by the force of gravitation, but when he does succeed in rising higher and higher through the circles of his spiralling prose, borne aloft like a glider on warm currents of air,

even today the reader is overcome by a sense of levitation. The greater the distance, the clearer the view: one sees the tiniest of details with the utmost clarity. (*RS* 19)

Levitation thus stands as the indispensable counterpart to melancholia throughout Sebald's literary and critical writings. Not only does it lift the burden of melancholia from the individual but also appears as an antecedent to redemption. Therefore, as Sebald strongly felt, melancholia should not be confused with numbing depression but rather be seen positively as a source of creativity.

*

The country estate of Somerleyton, 'imperceptibly nearing the brink of dissolution and silent oblivion' (*RS* 36), is the narrator's first port of call. While the majority of visitors arrive in the private comfort of their cars, he takes a shabby train from Norwich station and has 'to climb the wall like some interloper and struggle through the thicket' (*RS* 45) to reach the stately home. Throughout *The Rings of Saturn*, the narrator positions his solitary approach to country rambling against the habits of modern tourism. As the solitary walker knows full well, 'every foot traveller incurs the suspicion of the locals, especially nowadays, and particularly if he does not fit the image of a local rambler' (*RS* 175). At Somerleyton, the narrator reacts to tourist attractions like the miniature train with disdain. His focus lingers instead on easily-overlooked details: 'a solitary Chinese quail, evidently in a state of dementia, running to and fro along the edge of the cage and shaking its head every time it was about to turn, as if it could not comprehend how it had got into this hopeless fix' (*RS* 36). Empathetic solidarity with living things in cages is a thematic link between all of Sebald's works; Somerleyton provides another impressive example in the stuffed polar bear in the entrance hall: 'With its yellowish and moth-eaten fur, it resembles a ghost bowed by sorrow' (*RS* 36).[2]

While the present Lord Somerleyton (who bears the ancient royal title of 'Her Majesty The Queen's Master of the Horse') is treated with satirical distance, the narrator strikes up a conversation with a gardener who admits to having had a schoolboy fascination with the British bombing campaigns against Nazi Germany. Arriving in Germany in the 1950s as a member of the army, he was puzzled by the collective amnesia regarding the devastating atrocities wreaked upon the civil population: 'No one seemed to have written about their experiences or afterwards recorded their memories. Even if you asked people directly, it was as if everything had been erased from their minds' (RS 39). This forgetfulness, symptomized by a pervasive silence among his compatriots on the destruction of German cities, had occupied Sebald since the early 1980s. The reasons for the collective taboo would constitute the subject of his Zurich lectures on air war and literature in 1997–8 that were published a year later as *On the Natural History of Destruction*.

The next leg of his journey takes the narrator to the coastal town of Lowestoft. He is disheartened to notice the ubiquitous signs of decay and economic depression and attributes them to 'the hardline capitalist years of Baroness Thatcher' (RS 41):

> Nowadays, in some of the streets almost every other house is up for sale; factory owners, shopkeepers and private individuals are sliding ever deeper into debt; week in, week out, some bankrupt or unemployed person hangs himself; nearly a quarter of the population is now practically illiterate, and there is no sign of an end to the encroaching misery. (RS 42)

Sebald had always been an outspoken critic of Thatcherite politics, particularly the radical restructuring of the British higher education system. This quote, however, represents one of the rare cases where his very firm opinions on politics became manifest in a literary text rather than in personal conversation.

*

The episode set in a run-down coastal hotel in Lowestoft, concerning a fish so badly prepared it proves unfit for human consumption, functions as a humorous prelude to a more contentious link that Sebald constructs in the third chapter. Spotting a group of local fisherman at the coastline inspires the narrator to speculate philosophically about their desire 'to be in a place where they have the world behind them, and before them nothing but emptiness' (RS 52). This conjecture provides the cue for an eccentric 'natural history of the herring' that combines fact with fiction; the illustration on page 57, for example, only purports to show a herring: in fact, it is a cod.

The dramatic decline of the herring population through overfishing not only offers an example of man's exploitative attitude towards nature: it also emblematizes the genocides mankind wrought upon itself. To this end, Sebald brings up a certain Major George Wyndham Le Strange – whose initials tellingly recall Sebald's own. Le Strange, the reader is invited to assume, must have come across the horrible scene shown on a double-spread photo which depicts a pile of human corpses near the concentration camp at Bergen Belsen. This shocking image is linked to a postcard of the Lowestoft fish market a few pages earlier, representing the 'untold millions of herrings' (*RS* 55) that the now moribund city once harvested in its economic prime. The coincidence is all too evident without being made explicit; it falls to the reader to evaluate and take a position towards this provocative combination of the two images. Is this just an uncanny parallel? Or must we comprehend both piles of dead bodies as signifiers for the depressing fact that history is nothing but an endless repetition of slaughter, destruction, annihilation and catastrophe?

The photo from Bergen Belsen also relates to the next image inserted in the text, ostensibly a clipping from the local Norwich newspaper *Eastern Daily Press* relating the news of the death of Major Le Strange.[3] In fact, as the very eccentric habits of the former military man suggest, the article is a fake, and as such casts doubt on the authenticity of the picture taken at the liberation of Bergen Belsen. After all, it could very well be a photo of dead Germans, or, for that matter, have no relation at all to the Second World War. The dead bodies are not even visible underneath the blankets covering them, and the dense forest obscures the scene altogether. In this instance, however, the photo is indeed authentic, taken by a British photographer in the area of the camp where women and children were kept. All this is to highlight Sebald's strategic deployment of illustrations: they are not meant to clarify but obfuscate, questioning the traditional relation between word and image, as well as undermining a 'literal legibility' of his texts.

*

Picturesque Southwold provides the next setting for Sebald's reflections on war as a major element of the natural history of destruction. Sitting on a bench near Gunhill, the narrator gazes onto the sea and tries to re-imagine the dreadful Battle of Sole Bay in May 1672. However, he knows full well that 'the agony that was endured and the enormity of the havoc wrought defeat our powers of comprehension' (*RS* 78). Visiting the historic Sailor's Reading Room, Sebald's favourite retreat in Southwold, the narrator comes across a photographic history of the First World War published in 1933 (the year of Hitler's ascension to power):

> Every theatre of war is documented in this compendious collection, from the Vall'Inferno on the Austro-Italian Alpine front to Flanders fields. There are illustrations of all conceivable forms of violent death . . . , corpses rotting in the no-man's-land between the trenches, woodlands razed by artillery fire, battleships sinking under black clouds of petroleum smoke, armies on the march, never-ending streams of refugees, shattered zeppelins, scenes from Prszemysl and St Quentin, from Montfaucon and Gallipoli, scenes of destruction, mutilation, desecration, starvation, conflagration, and freezing cold. (*RS* 94)

Passages like this display Sebald's intention to generate a ritualistic effect by means of repetitive prosody that does not just intellectually persuade but also emotionally affect his readers. The havoc wreaked by the Great War – the seminal catastrophe of the twentieth century – in fact paved the way for the industrialized genocide of the Second World War. Accordingly, Sebald recounts the horrific mass murders and methods of torture as employed by the Croatian militias during the early 1940s in Bosnia. The atrocities, presented in all detail, are likely to shock the reader.[4] One can assume that Sebald's reason for bringing them in was to make the connection to the civil war in former Yugoslavia during the early 1990s when the book was written.

That history has a destructive tendency to repeat itself is an insight Sebald wants to stress in *The Rings of Saturn*. To this end, he unfolds a terrifying scenario stretching over centuries, comprised of countless battles on land, in the air and under the sea; deportations, ethnic cleansing, and genocide; and, last but not least, ultra-chauvinistic nationalism. The chamber of horrors of European history is in turn refracted through the atrocities committed by the imperial campaigns waged beyond the continent's borders. All of this confirms, once again, the belief, inherited by Sebald from Benjamin, that history is nothing but a succession of catastrophes.

When the focus shifts to the crimes perpetrated by the Belgians in the Congo in the fifth chapter, Sebald incorporates two biographical portraits into his book: Joseph Conrad and Roger Casement. Both men were profoundly troubled by the horrendous crimes committed during the 'opening' of the Congo. Conrad, like Sebald an emigrant to Britain, wrote his most famous text on the corruption wrought by the dream of Empire upon both the colonized and the colonizer. Not coincidently, there are a number of echoes between Conrad's *Heart of Darkness* (1899) and *The Rings of Saturn*. Sebald highlights Conrad's moral awareness 'that his own travails did not absolve him from the guilt which he had incurred by his mere presence in the Congo' (*RS* 120). This serves not only to judge those so-called 'fellow travellers' (like his parents) during the Nazi era in Germany; what is also implied is his conviction that we all are accumulating a degree of guilt merely by existing within the machine of Western civilization, and its relentless drive to exploit the weak and destroy our natural environment.

Casement's life offers a rare act of political sabotage. The British diplomat publicly denounced the bestial outrages in the Congo and other colonies, and paid the ultimate price for his disloyalty. Stubbornly opposing anything he saw as injustice, he later devoted his energies to Irish independence, and was finally executed in 1916 for high treason. Casement's resistance to the status quo stirs the obvious sympathy of the narrator, who, incidentally demonstrates his penchant for the provocative, when he makes the claim that the atrocities committed by the Belgian Crown, during the age of imperialism, resulted in bodily and mental deformations of modern-day Belgians: 'I well recall that on my first visit to Brussels in December 1964 I encountered more hunchbacks and lunatics than normally in a whole year' (*RS* 122–3).

Yet another example of Sebald's unconventional worldview is furnished by his implications about the Holocaust. The ruthless exploitation of the Congo, accompanied by the systematic enslavement and murder of the population, bear all too obvious similarities to what the Nazis did to European Jewry. This tacitly underlines Sebald's contentious view that the Holocaust is not a singular, incommensurable event, but part of a recurrent chain of disasters that mark the natural history of destruction.

*

As if more proof were needed, the sixth chapter occupies itself with yet another episode in the history of human self-destruction, namely the civil war that raged in southern China during the 1850s and 1860s. As so often, it is an authentic yet easily overlooked detail that catches the attention of the narrator, and then leads him to cross for the first time, a vast geographic distance in order to connect the apparently unconnected. In this instance it is the claim that the carriages used on a railway line between Southwold and Halesworth were originally built for a Chinese emperor.

The hidden connection between Suffolk and China conjures up the extremely violent history of the Taiping Rebellion. Led by the messianic Hung Hsiu-Ch'üan, a seemingly invincible army of holy warriors massacred their opponents. The narrator reminds his readers that 'more than twenty million died in just fifteen years. The bloody horror in China at that time went beyond all imagining' (*RS* 140). Its terrible climax was finally reached when the besieged leader took his life and several hundreds of thousand of his devotees followed suit:

> They committed self-slaughter in every conceivable way, with swords and with knives, by fire, by hanging, or by leaping from the rooftops and towers. Many are even said to have buried themselves alive. The mass suicide of the Taipingis is without historical parallel. (*RS* 141)

This collective suicide vividly exemplifies the auto-destructive force that Sebald believed to be the driving force behind the natural history of destruction.

The gory story of the rebels is complemented on the part of the ruling class by the case of Tz'u-hsi, the power-hungry dowager empress who rose to power a few years before the end of the Taiping Rebellion. According to the narrator, she ruled the country with an insatiable 'craving for absolute power, which grew more ruthless with every year that passed' (*RS* 149). Here we can see a clear reference to the theory of power developed by Elias Canetti in his seminal study *Crowds and Power* (1960), which

Sebald much admired. As Canetti shows in his study, the craving for power is underwritten by a deep paranoia which forces the sovereign to seek out the death of as many people as possible, in order to overcome the fear of losing his or her power – a fear that increases in proportion with the expansion of power itself. 'The more ostentatious the demonstrations of her authority became,' the narrator says about Tz'u-hsi, 'the more the fear of losing the infinite power she had so insidiously acquired grew within her' (RS 150). As roughly ten million of her subjects perish in a drought – causing parents to exchange 'children because they could not bear to watch the dying torment of their own' (RS 151) – the Dowager Empress cares only about providing enough food for her silkworms: 'Of all living creatures, these curious insects alone aroused a strong affection in her' (RS 151).[5]

The crucial role these insects play in *The Rings of Saturn* will be evident later in the text. At this point we should note that a coincidence provides once again a means by which Sebald can traverse the dimensions of space and time, by means of association. The ruthless Tz'u-hsi is contrasted to the poet Algernon Charles Swinburne, whose life, coincidentally, 'was coterminous to the year with that of the Dowager Empress' (RS 161). Despite his privileged background, Swinburne never pursued wealth, power or influence, things he despised, as the narrator notes with apparent approval. Due to physical ailments, he had to forego the romantic idea of a military career and the corresponding heroic death that awaited him on the battlefield. Instead, he 'devote(d) himself unreservedly to literature and thus, perhaps, to a no less radical form of self-destruction' (RS 163).

Writing as a form of self-annihilation is a theme that runs throughout Sebald's critical and literary texts. It features in essays on Peter Weiss and Robert Walser, Jean Améry, Chateaubriand and Rousseau, amongst others. And keeping in mind the exhausting and arduous labour that went into both the composition and promotion of *Austerlitz*, it becomes all too evident that Sebald himself finally fell prey to this tragic affliction.

*

Contrary to what the narrator claims, East Anglia was never subject to the kind of slash-and-burn destruction of forests he asserts in the beginning of the seventh chapter. This fabrication is used to stress the more general point developed at this stage, namely to identify civilization with the destructive force of fire: 'Our spread over the earth was fuelled by reducing the higher species of vegetation to charcoal, by incessantly burning whatever would burn' (*RS* 170). This principle extends to today and is at the heart of our technological advancement:

> Combustion is the hidden principle behind every artefact we create. From the earliest times, human civilization has been no more than a strange luminescence growing more intense by the hour, of which no one can say when it will begin to wane and when it will fade away. (*RS* 170)

The natural history of destruction is understood here as a burnout process which will eventually reduce the world to embers and ashes. Connecting this idea with the destructive role that combustion played in the Max Ferber story, Sebald forges a link between the Holocaust and the overall development of civilization. What is thereby implied, at least from a German perspective, is subtly provocative in two ways. Firstly, as we have seen before, the Nazi genocide is not a unique aberration but a prototypic indication of the downward slope of human evolution. Secondly, the Holocaust seems to be put on similar footing with the mass killings of German civilians by the Allied bombing campaign which caused hitherto unseen firestorms of disastrous consequence.

It goes without saying that the passage in which the narrator recounts how he erratically criss-crosses Dunwich Heath is meant to be read metaphorically: Despite signposts, he 'loses his way' and does not make 'any progress' but finds himself 'walking in circles' – a clear nudge towards a philosophy of history that contradicts any teleological idea of advancement towards a better future. What awaits us in future is signified by the vision of a 'solitary old man with a wild mane of hair kneeling beside his dead daughter' (*RS* 174) – who is, of course, none other than King Lear: 'Nothing but dead silence. Then softly, barely audibly, the sound of a funeral march' (*RS* 175).

In the village of Middleton, the narrator makes what is

probably his most important stopover when he visits 'the writer Michael Hamburger, who has lived there for almost twenty years' (RS 175). Sebald and Hamburger were connected by a close friendship, not least because they both shared the experience of being German immigrants to England, albeit in different ways. The story about Hamburger's escape from Nazi prosecution in 1933 as recounted in *The Rings of Saturn* is based largely on his autobiography *String of Beginnings* (1991); as always, Sebald adapts the source text to his purposes where necessary. The main parallel between Hamburger and Sebald is obvious – both men worked as academics but produced striking literary texts as well. However, there is one crucial difference: while Hamburger fully assimilated into English as his working language, Sebald remained ensconced in his native tongue.[6] Living on a kind of linguistic island this allowed him to write a peculiar German much unlike the rest of his contemporaries in German letters. And while Hamburger severed all ties with the land of his birth, Sebald retained his soft southern German accent as a remnant of the world he left behind.

The narrator goes to great lengths to stress the uncanny coincidences that connect his biography with that of his predecessor. He notes odd concurrences like the fact that both men had lived in Manchester and, in 1944 and 1966 respectively, met the same university lecturer. Puzzled, he asks us to consider:

> Across what distances in time do the elective affinities and correspondences connect? How is it that one perceives oneself in another human being, or, if not oneself, then one's own precursor? The fact that I first passed through British customs thirty-three years after Michael, that I am now thinking of giving up teaching as he did, that I am bent over my writing in Norfolk and he in Suffolk, that we both are distrustful of our work and both suffer from an allergy to alcohol – none of these things are particularly strange. But why it was that on my first visit to Michael's house I instantly felt as if I lived or had once lived there, in every respect precisely as he does, I cannot explain. (RS 182–3)

Sebald harnesses this moment of *déjà vu* to foster an identification between the narrator and a victim of Nazi persecution to a degree he had beforehand shied away from. Here indeed he invokes a bond that could be perceived as a symbolic restoration of the German-Jewish cultural symbiosis that was so violently severed by the Nazis.

*

In the eighth chapter, the narrator's visit to the extraterritorial zone of Orfordness, a site where the Ministry of Defence had conducted secret experiments during the Cold War, takes centre stage. Toying with the appeal of conspiracy theories, Sebald alludes to unsubstantiated stories about 'a horrifying incident' involving a kind of massive flame-throwing device that was kept secret despite eye witnesses 'who claimed to have seen the charred bodies, contorted with pain, lying on the beach or still out at sea in their boats' (RS 231). These rumours act as an unsettling prelude to what the narrator expects to find on 'the other side' of the now deserted area.

Without a doubt, the boat crossing from the mainland to Orfordness evokes Charon taking the narrator across the river Styx to the realm of dead souls. His first encounter in the deserted territory is with a frightened hare that runs away into a field as the solitary human approaches:

> It must have been cowering there as I approached, heart pounding as it waited, until it was almost too late to get away with its life. In that very fraction of a second when its paralysed state turned into panic and flight, its fear cut right through me. I still see what occurred in that one tremulous instant with an undiminished clarity. I see the edge of the grey tarmac and every individual blade of grass, I see the hare leaping out of its hiding-place, with its ears laid back and a curiously human expression on its face that was rigid with terror and strangely divided; and in its eyes, turning to look back as it fled and almost popping out of its head with fright, I see myself, become one with it. (RS 234–5)

Once more, Sebald creates a remarkable literary passage, an epiphanic glimpse of an individual released from the straitjacket of everyday perception, who intensively experiences a mystical union with an otherwise inaccessible 'other'.

Located in an ambiguous state between nature and civilization, present and past, there is a part of Orfordness where the former buildings have fallen into disrepair as nature reconquers the space that was temporarily abused by man for his misguided experiments. Accordingly, the decaying structures remind the

83

narrator of prehistoric graves: '(T)he closer I came to these ruins, the more any notion of a mysterious isle of the dead receded, and the more I imagined myself amidst the remains of our own civilization after its extinction in some future catastrophe' (*RS* 237). In what could be called an ontological flickering, this vision of a world that has already witnessed its ultimate catastrophe, poses one vexing question: what if the apocalypse has already taken place, unbeknown to us, who deceive ourselves in the futile belief that it can still be avoided?

*

The model of the Temple of Jerusalem that the narrator visits in the next chapter serves as an implicit poetological model for *The Rings of Saturn*. What fascinates him about the miniature temple is the passion of its builder, his dedication to detail, and his autodidactic approach. Abrams is a *bricoleur* par excellence – someone who follows his own designs rather than received orthodoxy. 'I don't consider myself a writer', Sebald once told an interviewer, 'It's like someone who builds a model of the Eiffel Tower out of matchsticks. It's a devotional work. Obsessive' (*EM* 169).

Hallmarks of literary *bricolage* abound in Sebald's works. One need only look to the arrangement of heterogeneous texts in *After Nature* or *Vertigo*, the intertextual weaving of his own words with unmarked quotations from other writers, the often experimental inclusion of illustrations in his texts or the unorthodox method of digressive association or inclusion of extremely long lists. And one more important thing: those Sebald readers who idolize him as a literary Messiah should heed the reply that Abrams gave to an evangelical Christian who asked him if the accurateness of the temple model was a result of divine revelation: 'No, it's just research really and work, endless hours of work' (*RS* 245). What better way to summarize the literary triumph that is *The Rings of Saturn*?

Chapter 9 concludes with an episode the significance of which is usually overlooked. The photo that shows Sebald in front of a tree should delight obedient readers who enjoy (con)fusing author with narrator. The latter discusses the devastating effects of the Dutch elm disease that spread from 1975 in East Anglia: 'The six elm trees which had shaded the pond in our garden withered away in June 1978, just a few weeks after they unfolded their marvellous light green foliage for the last time' (*RS* 264). What is remarkable about the few pages that Sebald dedicates to the arboreal scourge is the empathy with which the narrator talks about the trees as if they were human beings who were 'dying of thirst' (*RS* 264) and subject to 'near complete extermination', as the original German says with a clear overtone that is regrettably missing in the translation. The narrator is literally traumatized by a 'hurricane such as no one had ever experienced before' (*RS* 265), which he had to witness in October 1987. Looking out of his window, an unsettling view unveils itself before him, 'a formless scene that bordered upon the underworld. And at the very moment...I knew that everything down there had been destroyed' (*RS* 266). Inevitably, the uprooted trees on the ground conjure up the earlier photograph of the corpses scattered amongst tree trunks. This in turn puts the narrator into the position of Major Le Strange, the overwhelmed eyewitness to a shocking scene: 'For a long time I stood choked with emotion amidst the devastation' (*RS* 267), he confides.

Illustration 8: Storm devastation in 1987, photo taken by Sebald

85

Unlike many other seemingly real events that make their way into his works, both the storm and the devastation of Sebald's garden are authentic. And as an avid reader of Benjamin, Sebald could not but associate the storm with the famous ninth thesis *On the Philosophy of History*, in which the angel of history is propelled, helplessly, over a never-ending scene of devastation that we call the past, and into the future. 'This storm,' Benjamin concludes, 'is what we call progress.'[7]

*

In the final chapter Sebald closes the circle by returning to the writings of Thomas Browne. What has become clear by now are the close affinities of *The Rings of Saturn* to Browne's ambivalent view of the world, which unites reason and myth, scientific research and metaphysical speculation, local and cosmological components. Similarly, Sebald embeds inconspicuous things such as a crumbling windmill in East Anglia within a natural history of destruction, or associates natural catastrophes with modern mass murder. No surprise then that reading the book can result in a feeling of being trapped in one of the labyrinths that feature so prominently.

Browne's casual mention of the illicit trade in silkworms provides the cue for an idiosyncratic treatise of sericulture that turns out to be an implicit discussion, soon after, of the Holocaust. One aspect of this history that particularly interests the narrator is the role of sericulture under National Socialism. In 1936 Hitler ordered concerted efforts regarding the cultivation of silkworms, and the Nazis also considered sericulture of didactic benefit as school pupils could be taught 'the essential measures which are taken by breeders to monitor productivity and selection, including extermination to pre-empt racial degeneration' (*RS* 294). All too evidently, such language mirrors the racial policies of the fascists and their social Darwinist obsession with racial purity. Sebald takes this information from the supplement to a documentary film that was shown to schoolchildren like himself in the years after the war. What is communicated here is the unease about the subliminal continuation of fascist patterns of thought well after the demise of the Nazis: a tendency that Sebald also saw at work in many books published by German authors in the newly emerged

Federal Republic and which he duly castigated in his critical writings.

His efforts were directed at coming up with a new type of writing that would address the horrors of the German past but also place them in an overarching matrix, in order to enable a more insightful understanding of how our own existence is inextricably linked with that of other creatures and the natural world around us. Nowhere in his small body of work, cut short by an all too premature death, did he succeed better at this task than in *The Rings of Saturn*.

6

<hr />

Austerlitz (2001)

> I fear I still have grave doubts about the book.
>
> (Sebald on *Austerlitz* in a letter to Anthea Bell, June 2000)

Contrary to widely-held opinion, *Austerlitz* is a problematic book. In *Austerlitz*, for the first time Sebald veered dangerously close to the conventions of the novel, a form of writing he repeatedly disavowed in interviews. Classifying *Austerlitz* as 'a prose book of an undetermined kind' *(EM* 123) or 'a long prose elegy' *(EM* 103) did not prevent both critics and the general readership from perceiving it as a novel. As the book evolves around the reconstruction of the central character's life story, it is marked by a narrative coherence absent from his previous books. One very obvious manifestation of this unity can be seen in that *Austerlitz* is firmly focused on the title character, while all his other texts are collections of separate yet interrelated individual stories.

One of the reasons that Sebald resisted the categorization 'novel' was because it implied a narrative that was fictional in nature. Sebald, however, wanted *Austerlitz* to appear as an authentic tale of racist persecution; the title character, he maintained in interviews, is based on two real biographies. First, there is the supposed retired architectural historian from London of Czech origin. The 'picture of the child cavalier' *(A* 260), which features on both German and English cover of the book (and in other editions as well) is, according to Sebald, a photo of him as a five-year-old boy. However, it is telling that this person has thus far not been identified. Moreover, Sebald most probably acquired the photo, which is now amongst his papers in the German Literature Archive, at a rummage sale.[1]

Sebald's statements on *Austerlitz* require disobedient reading, too. In all likelihood, the architectural historian was invented in order to deflect attention from the second and indeed major model upon which the title character was constructed.[2] Susi Bechhöfer was born in Munich in 1936 to a Jewish mother and a German soldier father; in 1939, she and her twin sister, Lotte, were evacuated to safety in the United Kingdom. She recounts the story of the recovery of her origins in her memoir *Rosa's Child* (1996).[3] Sebald adopted several important aspects of her life for *Austerlitz*, such as her unhappy upbringing in the home of a Welsh preacher, and the unexpected discovery of her hidden identity as a result of a school headmaster casually informing her of her legal name.

Upon the publication of *Austerlitz*, Sebald asserted that he always obtained permission before utilizing biographies for literary purposes. This was not true with regard to *Austerlitz*. When Bechhöfer, who now lives as a retired nurse in Rugby, came across the novel, she was understandably upset about the unauthorized use of her story and asked that her name would be acknowledged in the book as a vital source of the narrative. In a letter dated 2 July 2001, Sebald wrote to her, expressing his hope 'that you approve of the way in which I have employed elements of your biography'. He admits that 'I was deeply moved by what you have been through' and explains that his aim was not to appropriate her life-story but 'to construct something like an exemplary case, at the remove of documented reality'. Sebald's premature death, however, prevented a personal meeting between them and Bechhöfer's story, as a crucial source for the book, still remains unacknowledged.[4]

Austerlitz is probably the point of entry to Sebald's *œuvre* for most readers, particularly so in the Anglophone world. One could even go so far as to say that the novel acts as the most likely initiation into the cult of Sebald (which will be examined in the next chapter). For the first time Sebald directly engaged the Nazi genocide, unlike in *The Emigrants*, where it looms in the background. In a sense, this move backfired, because one of the consequences was Sebald's unwanted categorization as a 'Holocaust author' in the Anglophone world. This could be one of the reasons for the reservations about the novel he expressed in private, notably in correspondence with the book's English translator, Anthea Bell.

Critics in Germany were largely divided about the novel. On the one hand, a few major critics reacted to *Austerlitz* with a general sense of unease, denouncing Sebald as a purveyor of 'melancholic kitsch' or lambasting the connection between staghorn buttons in a Terezín junkshop and the Holocaust, which they saw as trivializing the Shoah. The fact that Sebald relegated the narrator to the role of mouthpiece for the title character was met with conflicting response. While some critics welcomed the priority accorded to a victim of the Holocaust, others attacked Sebald for what they saw as a Gentile appropriating Jewish suffering. Sceptical voices in the English-speaking world, on the other hand, were few and far between. Arthur Lubow, for example, correctly sensed that in *Austerlitz* 'the author's unconventional mind is creaking against the walls of convention' (*EM* 169). Or when Michael Hofmann denounced the book as 'trite' and maintained that 'perhaps a nineteenth-century ready-made fog' (*EM* 91) emanates from it, he clearly set out to provoke. Nevertheless, some provocation is welcome as a corrective, when thinking about a book that has received almost universal praise in the Anglophone world.

In any case, it should be mentioned that Sebald redeploys a number of narrative tricks, tropes and motifs from his previous texts in *Austerlitz*, sometimes less successfully. What works in a disjointed narrative framework like *Vertigo*, namely the abundance of unlikely coincidences, functions less smoothly in an apparently more realistic novel like *Austerlitz*. For instance, it seems almost impossible that Austerlitz could have remained unaware of the Jewish cemetery adjacent to his East London home. Finally, it needs to be said that Sebald occasionally fails to maintain the narrative thrust to drive a mostly non-linear plot stretched over more than four hundred pages. Maybe because he was accustomed to writing stories of no more than a hundred pages?

*

Despite the fact that *Austerlitz* does not qualify as the untouchable masterpiece that many critics declare it to be, it nevertheless represents a truly landmark moment in contemporary literature. The story begins in 1967 at Antwerp's Centraal Station, whose architectural grandeur appears to the uneasy narrator as a reflection of the colonial crimes of the previous century. Through a succession of streets whose names allude to salvation and redemption, he makes his way to the nocturama of the local zoo. The inmates of this 'topsy-turvy miniature universe' (*A* 4) lead 'sombrous lives behind the glass by the light of a pale moon' (*A* 2) and arouse feelings of pity and creaturely empathy in the narrator. What commands his particular attention is a raccoon who is

> washing the same piece of apple over and over again, as if it hoped that all this washing, which went far beyond any reasonable thoroughness, would help it to escape the unreal world in which it had arrived, so to speak, through no fault of its own. (*A* 2–3)

As attentive readers will realize, the poor creature's condition reflects the tragic life story of Jacques Austerlitz. We are first introduced to the title character when the narrator turns his attention from the animals to the strange man 'occupied in making notes and sketches' (*A* 6) of the Centraal Station. For reasons that are unclear even to himself, the narrator approaches him and strikes up a conversation that ends up extending late into the night. The enigmatic scholar states that, in pursuing his research on power structures as manifested in 'the architectural style of the capitalist era', he is 'obeying an impulse which he himself... did not really understand' (*A* 44).

Austerlitz's research project on the 'architectural style of the bourgeois era' bears many traits of Benjamin's interest in nineteenth-century monumentalism as a symptom of the triumphant spirit of capitalism. Antwerp Station, Austerlitz observes, is built like 'a cathedral consecrated to international traffic and... the deities of the nineteenth century – mining, industry, transport, trade, and capital' (*A* 12–13). The two pillars of this new age, according to Austerlitz, are the precise measurement of time and the expansion of the railway network. Readers learn later of the entangled connection between Austerlitz's life and railways; as in the case of Bereyter, the Holocaust looms in the background of his 'obsession with railway stations' (*A* 45). With reference to Claude Lanzmann's *Shoah* (1985), Sebald once explained: 'The railway played a very, very prominent part, as we know, in the process of deportation.... The whole logistics of deportation was based on the logistics of the railway system' (*EM* 53).

Concerning chronometry, Sebald provides a demonstration of his writerly talents in the description of the mighty yet somewhat shabby clock that quite literally towers over the station buffet:

> During the pauses in our conversation we both noticed what an endless length of time went by before another minute had passed, and how alarming seemed the movement of that hand, which resembled a sword of justice, even though we were expecting it every time it jerked forward, slicing off the next one-sixtieth of an hour from the future and coming to a halt with such a menacing quiver that one's heart almost stopped. (*A* 8–9)

This remarkable sentence contains central themes of the book such as transience, threat or death. It pinpoints the crucial idea of hindering the flow of time and culminates, with typical Sebald hyperbole, in one of the key metaphors of *Austerlitz*: the broken, damaged, arrested heart.

The main subject of the first chance encounter between the narrator and Austerlitz concerns the history of military fortification. Austerlitz discusses the belt of fortifications around Antwerp and mentions in particular the fortress of Breendonk, 'completed just before the outbreak of the First World War in which, within a few months, it proved completely useless for the defence of the city and the country' (*A* 23). What draws the narrator to the ruin is the fact that the Germans used it as a penal camp from 1940, where prisoners were routinely subjected to torture in the gruesome casemate. Approaching the fort, it appears to him as a misshapen monstrosity 'so far exceeding my comprehension that in the end I found myself unable to connect it with anything shaped by human civilization, or even with the silent relics of our prehistory and early history' (*A* 26). This visit to the fort, not surprisingly, proves thought-provoking. The narrator can easily imagine the everyday life of the German guards and torturers, 'good fathers and dutiful sons from Vilsbiburg and Fuhlsbüttel, from the Black Forest and the Bavarian Alps, . . . after all, I had lived among them until my twentieth year' (*A* 29). The unspeakable fate of the inmates, however, eludes him entirely: 'I could not envisage the drudgery performed day after day, year after year, at Breendonk', where the prisoners were maltreated 'until their hearts nearly burst' (*A* 29).

What is at stake here is the question of how (or how not) to integrate unimaginable suffering into one's horizon of experience via the human facility of empathy. This difficult issue is explored in yet another *katabasis*, when the narrator enters the fortress and descends into an underworld 'cut off for ever from the light of nature' (*A* 30). The 'fourteen stations' (*A* 29) through which visitors to Breendonk must pass en route to the torture chamber are, of course, an allusion to the fourteen Stations of the Cross. Sebald is once more on controversial ground: entering the pit in which prisoners, including Jean Améry, were tortured, the narrator associates the torture chamber with both the laundry room of his childhood home and the blood-stained walls of the village butcher shop. For the narrator, these analogies are wrought with horror: 'No one can explain exactly what happens within us when the doors behind which our childhood terrors lurk are flung open' (*A* 33).

Another psychological 'hyperlink' is provoked by 'the nauseating smell of soft soap' pervading the fort, something that rekindles the memory of being scrubbed with a brush, along with the feelings of powerlessness, disgust and patriarchal supremacy. The psychosomatic reaction of dizziness in turn conjures up a sensation of the

> third-degree interrogations which were being conducted here around the time I was born, since it was only a few years later that I read Jean Améry's description of the dreadful physical closeness between torturers and their victims, and of the tortures he himself suffered in Breendonk when he was hoisted aloft by his hands, tied behind his back, so that with a crack and a splintering sound which, as he says, he had not yet forgotten when he came to write his account, his arms dislocated from the sockets in his shoulder joints, and he was left dangling as they were wrenched up behind him and twisted together above his head. (*A* 33–4)

This passage paraphrases Améry's autographical essay *Torture* (1966), in which he describes the ordeal as an experience of existential subjection and uncanny proximity between torturer and victim. Harrowing childhood cleansing rituals and torture are linked to overcome the distance between the narrator and Améry, a link strengthened by the fact they took place around the same time. Sebald's appropriation of Améry's life story – about whom he had written a number of incisive essays – in this more literary medium is, however, a daring gesture. As if rendering himself as a *doppelgänger* of Michael Hamburger in *The Rings of Saturn* wasn't enough, the narrator's assumption of the identity of a victim of Nazi persecution treads on morally precarious terrain. Though Sebald doubtlessly aims to demonstrate his solidarity with Améry, the obvious charge of misappropriating Jewish suffering raises its head, all the more justified given his origins. It ultimately falls to the reader to decide if such a gesture is permissible. In any case, this is not a problem unique to Sebald, but one of the most enduring questions regarding representations of the Holocaust in literature.

*

The passage dealing with Breendonk concludes what can be called the overture of *Austerlitz,* namely an introduction to the protagonist, the major themes and motifs, and its narrative framework. From this point onwards, the text unravels the tangled lines of Austerlitz's life, a disentanglement that takes place as a result of accidental meetings as 'our paths kept crossing, in a way that I still find hard to understand' (*A* 36). (Disobedient readers, too, might be sceptical of the frequency of these convergences across Europe.)

Their second meeting is set in a shabby tavern ambiguously called Café des Espérances, 'which no sensible person would have sought out' (*A* 37) while the next reunion takes place once 'again entirely by chance,... on the steps of the Palace of Justice' in Brussels. In contrast to the Parisian café, this landmark site, a 'building of singular architectural monstrosity, on which Austerlitz was planning to write a study at the time,' cannot be overlooked (*A* 38). Combining ideas from Benjamin's essay *Critique of Violence* (1921) with semi-fantastic images from Kafka's novel *The Trial* (1925), Austerlitz says that the immense structure looming ominously over the Belgian capital 'contains corridors and stairways leading nowhere, and doorless rooms and halls where no one would ever set foot, empty spaces surrounded by walls and representing the innermost secret of all sanctioned authority' (*A* 39).

The next improbable meeting between the narrator and Austerlitz happens on a ferry travelling between Holland and the United Kingdom, during which each learns that the other resides in England. The disciple-mentor relationship that develops between the two men recalls the intense bond between the narrator of *The Emigrants* and Paul Bereyter – 'Austerlitz was the first teacher I could listen to since my time in primary school' (*A* 43–4). Despite the intensity of their bond, they soon after lose touch. The narrator speculates that his migration back to his homeland is the culprit: 'I returned to Germany at the end of 1975, intending to settle permanently in my native country, to which I felt I had become a stranger after nine years of absence' (*A* 45). This statement aligns the narrator's story with Sebald's own biography. Likewise, the sudden onset of problems with his eyesight in December 1997 coincides with a similar affliction that befell Sebald at the same time. It is tempting to interpret this ailment as a psychosomatic response to the crisis that Sebald experienced when he failed to make progress with the Corsica project – the venture he abandoned in order to work on *Austerlitz*. It is surely the author speaking when the narrator says that he felt both 'concern for my ability to continue working and at the same time . . . a vision of release in which I saw myself, free of the constant compulsion to read and write, sitting in a wicker chair in a garden, surrounded by a world of indistinct shapes' (*A* 48). Seeking medical help from a specialist, the narrator travels to London where, once more, he accidently meets Austerlitz while waiting for a homebound train in a bar at Liverpool Street station. While observing the unpleasant spectacle of City employees boisterously guzzling their wages away, he 'suddenly noticed a solitary figure on the edge of the agitated crowd, a figure who could only be Austerlitz, whom I . . . had not seen for nearly twenty years' (*A* 54).

At this point in *Austerlitz*, the narrator notices a 'certain physical likeness between' the main character and the philosopher Wittgenstein: 'Whenever I see a photograph of Wittgenstein somewhere or other, I feel more and more as if Austerlitz were gazing at me out of it' (*A* 56).[5] What links the fictional character with the philosopher is the well-worn rucksack both men carry.[6] The backpack represents the existential homelessness and transitory presence of Austerlitz; as he himself will later comprehend, it is also a token of his participation in the *Kindertransports*, the name given to the series of rescue operations for 'non-Aryan' children from Nazi-occupied Europe.

It is in the Great Eastern Hotel that Austerlitz finally confides in the narrator: 'Since my childhood and youth... I have never known who I really was' (*A* 60). He grew up, as he explains, 'in the little country town of Bala in Wales, in the home of a Calvinist preacher and former missionary Emyr Elias' (*A* 61) in rather depressing circumstances. The preacher and his wife rechristened him Dafydd Elias, and obliterated his previous life in the hope of giving him a new start. The fact that 'several rooms on the top floor were kept shut up year in, year out' (*A* 61) mirrors the early memories of Austerlitz that remain locked in his mind, until one day the doors of recollection open up in an epiphany.

What he does remember, though, is the pain of having 'to face the knowledge, new every day, that I was not at home now but very far away, in some kind of captivity' (*A* 61–2). When he is sent to a private boarding school, Austerlitz finally finds a respite from the emotionally-dead climate of the Elias household. The summer of 1949 marks a turning point, when the headmaster discloses the unsettling truth that young Dafydd's real name is Jacques Austerlitz:

> All he knew was that the Eliases had taken me into their house at the beginning of the war, when I was only a little boy, so he could tell me no more.... As far as the other boys are concerned... you remain Dafydd Elias for the time being. There's no need to let anyone know. (*A* 94)

This disturbing revelation casts a pallor over most of his life, barring Austerlitz from sustaining any close relationships. This changes after the pivotal scene of revelation in the London bookshop that initiates Austerlitz's search for his real identity the Eliases laboured so hard to erase. However much Austerlitz remained ignorant of his 'own story' (*A* 43) for most of his life, there were nevertheless a number of hints along the way that suggested the existence of his obliterated prehistory. So much is evident from his obsession with analogue photography and the gradual processes of enlightenment in the darkroom:

> I was always especially entranced... by the moment when the shadows of reality, so to speak, emerge out of nothing on the exposed paper, as memories do in the middle of the night, darkening again if you try to cling to them, just like a photographic print left in the developing bath too long. (*A* 109)

Austerlitz shares his passion for photography with Gerald Fitzpatrick, the fag assigned to him when he enters the sixth form. The two quickly take a liking to each other, and Gerald invites Austerlitz to his family estate, Andromeda Lodge. One of the many extraterritorial sanctuaries and paradisiacal retreats that appear in Sebald's books, the Fitzpatrick home is characterized by an odd synthesis of nature and civilization 'that made you feel you were living in another world' (A 115).

Gerald's Great-Uncle Alphonso, plainly modelled on Sebald's grandfather, is particularly close to Austerlitz and introduces him 'into the mysterious world of moths' (A 127). Like the digressions about other marginal creatures such as the herring or the silk-worm in *The Rings of Saturn*, Sebald offers readers a kind of celebratory animal folklore through Alphonso and his passionate discourse on all the peculiarities and abilities of the species, easily winning his audience over: '(T)he two of us,' Austerlitz tells the narrator, 'Gerald and I, could not get over our amazement at the endless variety of these invertebrates, which are usually hidden from our sight' (A 128). Alphonso's loving entomological explications open Austerlitz's eyes to the life of insects overlooked and creatures mistreated. As Austerlitz affirms,

> there is really no reason to suppose that lesser beings are devoid of sentient life. We are not alone in dreaming at night for, quite apart from dogs and other domestic creatures whose emotions have been bound up with ours for many thousands of years, the smaller mammals such as mice and moles also live in a world that exists only in their minds whilst they are asleep, as we can detect from their eye movements. (A 133–4)

This passage confirms Eric Santner's observation that the 'creaturely' in Sebald's texts carries an ethical dimension that underwrites the moral dimension of his works. Alphonso's speculations about the 'secret life of animals' is both poetic and deeply steeped in early romantic German thought. Yet a disobedient reader might ask whether Sebald overplays his hand when philosophizing about dreaming insects and vegetables: 'who knows, said Austerlitz, perhaps moths dream as well, perhaps a lettuce in the garden dreams as it looks up at the moon by night' (A 133–4).

*

97

Time is an important theme in *Austerlitz*. Taking his cue from Benjamin, Sebald time and time again argues against received notions of temporality:

> Time, said Austerlitz..., was by far the most artificial of all our inventions, and in being bound to the planet turning on its own axis was no less arbitrary than would be, say, a calculation based on the growth of trees or the duration required for a piece of limestone to disintegrate. (*A* 141–2)

This stance against linear time not only undermines a major foundation of technological progress, it also opens up a metaphysical space that allows for the parallel existence of different time zones. Furthermore, questioning its hegemonic force in our imagination allows for the recollection of lost (including buried) histories, and ultimately challenges a corollary of time's iron-fisted reign: the irrevocability of death.

From this perspective, the area around Liverpool Street station offers the ideal terrain for Austerlitz's psycho-geographical excursions. After all, this site once housed 'the hospital for the insane and other destitute persons which has gone down in history under the name of Bedlam'. And for those who have the sensory capacity to register its presence, the past has not at all turned into history:

> I often wondered whether the pain and suffering accumulated on this site over the centuries had ever really ebbed away, or whether they might not still, as I sometimes thought when I felt a cold breath of air on my forehead, be sensed as we passed through them. (*A* 183)

After a mental breakdown forces him into early retirement in 1991, Austerlitz, for reasons that are no clearer to him than to the reader, compulsively begins to meander the streets of London at night. Like the animals in the nocturama, the normal pattern of waking and sleeping is reversed for this urban nomad. In the heightened state of aimless wandering, he is magnetically drawn to the train station which was 'one of the darkest and most sinister places in London, a kind of entrance to the underworld' (*A* 180).

During these journeys often his mind plays tricks on him. For example, he seems to 'hear people behind my back speaking in a foreign tongue, Lithuanian, Hungarian, or something else with a very alien note to it' (*A* 180). These ghostly apparitions are, obviously, the suppressed remnants of his lost Czech tongue. During one of these walks, Austerlitz sees a station porter wearing a white turban and follows him to the long disused Ladies Waiting Room, where he is overwhelmed with a surreal vision that is reminiscent of Piranesi's dreamlike architectural drawings:

> I saw huge halls open up, with rows of pillars and colonnades leading far into the distance, with vaults and brickwork arches bearing on them many-storied structures, with flights of stone steps, wooden stairways and ladders, all leading the eye on and on. I saw viaducts and footbridges crossing deep chasms thronged with tiny figures who looked to me, said Austerlitz, like prisoners in search of some way of escape from their dungeon. (*A* 190–1)

The peculiarity of this hallucination reveals Austerlitz's disposition to conceptualize his lost identity in architectural terms. That is, this imaginary room is a visualization of his mental 'interior', and the 'prisoners' unable to escape are a projection of his quest to uncover the hidden truth of his erased life.

More importantly, the Ladies Waiting Room is the setting for Austerlitz's crucial recollection of one specific and very important suppressed memory, namely his arrival in London on one of the *Kindertransports*: in this 'same waiting room I had come on my arrival in England over half a century ago' (*A* 193). Austerlitz visualizes his foster parents and 'the boy they had come to meet. He was sitting by himself on a bench over to one side . . . and but for the small rucksack he was holding on his lap I don't think I would have known him, said Austerlitz' (*A* 193).

Having now forcefully pried open the gates of memory, Austerlitz begins in earnest to unravel the riddle of his life. Pivotal to this archaeological investigation is yet another chance encounter. When browsing in a bookshop in Central London, he overhears a radio programme featuring two fellow members of the *Kindertransports*. These two women's recollections confirm the faint images of his own arrival, and provide the definitive proof that persuades him to travel to the Czech capital to research his biography. Through yet another set of rather unlikely events, he quickly locates his childhood home, which, against all odds, is still occupied by his childhood nanny, Věra, whose stories miraculously revive his lost Czech tongue. Asked to accept this highly unlikely scenario, the reader now learns the identity of little 'Jacquot', the opera singer Agáta Austerlitz, and his father, Maximilian Aychenwald, a prominent official of the Czech Social Democratic Party. There is little that the former nanny can tell Austerlitz about his father except that he fled to Paris when German troops invaded Prague; his son will later take up his trail in the French capital. His mother, Austerlitz learns, suffered under the anti-Semitic regime introduced by the Nazis and made frantic efforts to bring about her and her son's emigration: 'she stood for hours in the sole post office..., waiting to send a telegram; she made inquiries, pulled strings, left financial deposits, produced affidavits and guarantees, and when she came home she would sit up racking her brains until late into the night' (*A* 244).

She fails to find a way to save both their lives. She does, however, secure the safety of her five-year-old son by getting him a coveted seat on a *Kindertransport*. In winter 1942, two years after bidding farewell to her son, Věra reveals, Agáta is deported to the ghetto of Theresienstadt, from which, Austerlitz later establishes, she is 'sent east in September 1944 with one and a half thousand others' (*A* 287) to the gas chambers. At this point in her recollections, the nanny hands over the photo of young Austerlitz that adorns the book's cover. To Austerlitz, the photo is a disturbing confrontation with his former self, and he feels a request in 'the piercing, inquiring gaze of the page boy who had come to demand his dues, who was waiting in the grey light of dawn on the empty field for me to accept the challenge and avert the misfortune lying ahead of him' (*A* 260).

Replications of photographs also dominate the following passages which describe Austerlitz's exploration of Terezín, the garrison town that housed the ghetto Theresienstadt. 'The most striking aspect of the place,' he observes, 'was its emptiness, something which to this day I still find incomprehensible' (A 266). The unsettling nature of the scene is seemingly confirmed by the nearly dozen photographs Sebald himself snapped during a research trip to the village in April 1999. The images appear in the text in strikingly short succession and mostly depict dark windows and closed doors, creating a deep sense of desolation. One shows an 'ivory-coloured porcelain group of a hero on horseback' (*A* 276) shot through the window of the junk shop, ANTIKOS BAZAAR, a photo of particular significance for two reasons. Firstly, the reflection of the photographer on the window is faintly discernible, the author's ghostly presence literally confronting readers head-on in the middle of his final book. Secondly, there is the heroic knight on horseback 'turning to look back... in order to raise up with his outstretched left arm an innocent girl already bereft of her last hope, and to save her from a cruel fate not revealed to the observer' (A 276). This damsel in distress can only be Agáta, transforming the scene into an allegory for the irrational guilt that plagues Austerlitz for his inability to protect his mother from her murderers.

Walking through the former site of the ghetto, Austerlitz is haunted by the eerie feeling that the souls of all those who suffered a fate similar to that of his mother still inhabit the place. They are 'crammed into those buildings and basements and attics, as if they were incessantly going up and down the stairs, looking out of the windows, moving in vast numbers through the streets and alleys' (A 281). The surrealism of the scene is the hallmark of a mode of thinking that Sebald likes to evoke in his writings – the ambiguous grey zone between immanence and transcendence, past and present:

> It does not seem to me, Austerlitz added, that we understand the laws governing the return of the past, but I feel more and more as if time did not exist at all, only various spaces interlocking according to the rules of a higher form of stereometry, between which the living and the dead can move back and forth as they like, and the longer I think about it the more it seems to me that we who are still alive are unreal in the eyes of the dead, that only occasionally, in certain lights and atmospheric conditions, do we appear in their field of vision. (A 261)

Austerlitz leaves Terezín under circumstances that carry over-tones of an expulsion. Back in London, he suffers a catastrophic mental breakdown as a result of the confrontation with his mother's fate. Continuing his investigation, and as a therapeutic measure, he reads H. G. Adler's extensive eyewitness account of ghetto life. Using material provided by Adler, Sebald evokes the circumstances of life in the ghetto, which Adler renders in incredible detail, by way of a monstrous sentence that stretches over ten pages; the very successful and fluid transposition of it into English by the translator Anthea Bell represents a Herculean feat (A 331–42).

Austerlitz's search for his mother concludes when he finally manages to obtain an image of her. At first, he locates a woman resembling 'my dim memory of my mother' (A 353) in a Nazi propaganda film about Theresienstadt: 'She looks just as I imagined the singer Agáta from my faint memories and I gaze and gaze again at that face, which seems to me both strange and familiar' (A 351). But this picture turns out not to be of Agáta. A second image, this time of a similar-looking woman, taken from a theatrical archive in Prague, is confirmed to be her likeness by Věra. But what has been lost cannot be retrieved; of the dead, only the ghostly presence on photographs remains.

*

Having achieved a kind of closure, albeit qualified, in the quest for his mother, Austerlitz travels to Paris to look for traces of his father. The surprised narrator receives a postcard inviting him to visit Austerlitz at the latter's apartment in the Thirteenth Arrondissement – the last time the two will ever meet. Austerlitz regretfully informs the narrator that the search for his father has not unearthed any concrete results. What remains is only the futile hope, 'against all reason, that I might suddenly see my father appear out of nowhere, coming towards me or stepping out of an entrance' (A 358). Austerlitz uses the opportunity to tell the narrator about an earlier stay in Paris during the late 1950s working in the Bibliothèque Nationale. As always in Sebald's books, the library offers a site of refuge, although intellectual labour normally ends up resembling a form of serfdom. To use Austerlitz's own words: he was never sure if 'here in the reading room of the library, I was on the Islands of the Blest or, on the contrary, in a penal colony' (A 364–7).

It was in the Bibliothèque Nationale that Austerlitz first met Marie de Verneuil, the only woman ever to emotionally connect with him. She then stands by Austerlitz's side during his multiple hospitalizations, the psychosomatic symptoms of his inability to grasp his identity. 'At some time in the past,' he ponders, 'I must have made a mistake, and now I am living the wrong life' (A 298). It was also Marie who in 1972 suggested a trip to (the then) Czechoslovakian spa town of Marienbad in the hope of helping Austerlitz break through his isolation.

Rather than cure him, however, the ill-fated trip results in the couple's separation as Austerlitz inexplicably falls into an increasingly withdrawn and paranoid state of mind. He senses something extremely uncanny about the place; a secret that strongly besets him yet seems impossible to unravel. Later he finds out that his instincts were correct, for as a child he had vacationed in Marienbad with his parents. 'Something or other unknown wrenched at my heart here in Marienbad,' he says, 'something very obvious like an ordinary name or a term which one cannot remember for the sake of anyone or anything in the world' (A 300). Parting from Marie, he explains to the narrator, was his only way to deal with the desolate insight that his destiny had turned him 'into a frightful and hideous creature, a man beyond the pale' (A 304) – someone who cannot bond with other human beings.

The Bibliothèque Nationale features again in the concluding moments of the novel, as Austerlitz relates his failed attempts during the 1990s to learn more about his father's fate from the library's archives. Things have changed considerably since the early 1970s. Like its London equivalent, the Bibliothèque Nationale has migrated to a massive, hyper-modern structure exemplifying the worst kind of modern architecture. Sebald has Austerlitz denounce the monumental failure in truly polemical terms: 'Both in its outer appearance and inner constitution, (it is) unwelcoming if not inimical to human beings, and runs counter, on principle, one might say, to the requirements of any true reader' (A 386). He describes the library as a kind of fortress, 'which in both its entire layout and its near-ludicrous internal regulation seeks to exclude the reader as a potential enemy' (A 398). This passionate lament stems from Sebald's wholesale rejection of modern culture, and, furthermore, confirms the underlying theme of the natural history of destruction. Namely, that modern civilization is afflicted by a fatal flaw that also manifests itself in the complex systems fashioned to make living in such a mode feasible:

> I came to the conclusion that in any project we design and develop, the size and degree of complexity of the information and control systems inscribed in it are the crucial factors, so that the all-embracing and absolute perfection of the concept can in practice coincide, indeed ultimately must coincide, with its chronic dysfunction and constitutional instability. (A 392–3)

Near the end of his book, Sebald relies again on the principle of association and suggestion. The word Austerlitz, after all, stands in for many different things: a Bohemian village, a famous battle, a Paris train terminus and a fictional character. Of particular importance to Sebald is the link between the latter two and the traumatic history inscribed in this connection. He learns from a newspaper report that

> on the waste land between the marshaling yard of the Gare d'Austerlitz and the pont de Tolbiac where this Babylonian library now rises, there stood until the end of the war an extensive warehousing complex to which the Germans brought all the loot they had taken from the homes of the Jews of Paris. (A 401)

The monstrosity of the national library is thereby deemed to be an inheritor of the monstrous Nazi warehouse that preceded it. Furthermore, the nearby railway station, named after the great battle near the Czech village of Austerlitz, is the place from which his father must have departed as he fled the German invasion. On their last meeting, Austerlitz tells the narrator that he has just learned from the 'records center in the rue Geoffroy-l'Asnier, that Maximilian Aychenwald had been interned during the latter part of 1942 in the camp at Gurs, a place in the Pyrenean foothills which he, Austerlitz, must now seek out ' (A 404). With that plan, Austerlitz disappears from the narrator's sight and that of the readers'.

The fact that he hands over the keys to his house in London to the narrator implies that his journey will be one of no return. (And it provides a somewhat transparent explanation for the appearance of the many photos stemming from Austerlitz's possession throughout the book.) Closing the circle, the narrator once again travels to Antwerp to see the nocturama and Breendonk, though this time he does not dare to enter the fortress. Instead he reads Dan Jacobson's *Heshel's Kingdom* (1998), in which the South African-born author and former professor of English literature at University College London describes the painful, almost futile search for information on his Lithuanian Jewish grandfather.[7] The closeness of this story to the plot of *Austerlitz* is evident, as are the parallels between the two foreign academics teaching in England and writing literary books on the side. Heshel's life is prematurely cut short by his 'weak heart' (*A* 414), a fate Sebald himself shared. Just like Antwerp, the city of Kaunas features a ring of useless fortresses conscripted into the Nazi extermination machine. As Jacobson reports, one of the deportees inscribed the message '*Nous sommes neuf cents Français*' (*A* 415) on his prison wall. This obviously opens up the speculation that the fictional Aychenwald, who bears the same first name that Sebald coined for himself, might have been one of them.

Beyond Sebald's authorial control, however, is the authentic list of names quoted from Jacobson's book of those who perished in Kaunas: 'Lob, Marcel, de St. Nazaire; Wechsler, Abram, de Limoges; Max Stern, Paris, 18.5.44' (*A* 415). Again, Sebald's adopted first name features; uncannily, the Paris Jew also shared the first letter of his surname with the German writer from the Allgäu who, even more uncannily, was born on the very day that the doomed men left their names 'on the cold limestone wall of the bunker' (*A* 415).

The explanation of this mysterious coincidence, which as fate would have it, would prove to be Sebald's literary testament, also reads as a cryptic confirmation of an irrational awareness he always firmly maintained:

> I have slowly learned to grasp how everything is connected across space and time, ... dates of birth with dates of death, happiness with misfortune, natural history and the history of our industries, that of *Heimat* with that of exile. (*PC* 163)

7

The Cult of Sebald

For me, when I wrote my first texts, it was a very, very private affair. So the privacy which that ensured for me was something that I treasured a great deal, and it isn't so now. So my instinct is now to abandon it all again until people have forgotten about it, and then perhaps I can regain that position where I can work in my potting shed, undisturbed.

(Sebald in an interview with Eleanor Wachtel)

Amongst the myths surrounding Sebald, the most common misconception is the belief that *Austerlitz* was the last book published during his lifetime. Actually, *For Years Now*, a collection of short poetry, appeared just a few days before his death. However, the widely praised novel that placed him firmly on the short list for the Nobel Prize for Literature, has seemed to be the more fitting conclusion to the life story of a great writer cut tragically short.

Yet *For Years Now*, his collaboration with the British artist Tess Jaray, is an extraordinary book, which has been much undervalued. It combines short to very short poems by Sebald with monochrome patterns by Jaray. The volume thereby aims to break with several expectations Sebald's readers then had of his work: as well his first collaboration, it was his first published collection of poetry, and – this is a crucial point we will later return to – his one and only book written in English. In 1997 Sebald asserted in an interview that making the transition to writing in a foreign language 'is a very, very risky and harrowing decision. And so far I have tried to avoid making that decision' (*EM* 51). Yet taking risky decisions, deviating from the prescribed path and coming up with books unlike the ones that came before is very much characteristic of a wilful side of

Sebald that is rarely acknowledged. Following the long novel, strewn with his trademark grainy black and white images, *For Years Now* delivers dense, enigmatic poetic vignettes and vivid, colour-intense plates, making it at odds with its popular predecessor. Sebald was not one for the limelight and despised public appearances – speaking at less than a handful of literary readings in the United Kingdom. Similarly, interviews were viewed as a necessary evil. His revenge, in a way, was to not correct interviewers' wrong assumptions, such as 'Max/imilian' being his given middle name rather than a self-chosen one. Once brought into the world, such myths acquired a life of their own; for example, he was always said to have had a chair in Modern German Literature, when in fact it was in European Literature.

Sebald, it appears, is already established as a literary brand name, and his texts have increasingly become a point of reference and even a touchstone for judging the books of other writers. Quite a few aspiring writers are choosing to imitate his style and themes, some blatantly, others more subtly so.[1] The recent craze for books intertwining text and images in the Anglophone world is only one indicator of the wide-reaching cultural influence of his writing.[2] There are all sorts of examples of the way in which Sebald is appropriated for causes he would not really have identified with. Apart from the misplaced label as a Holocaust author, he would have witnessed with no less horror the literary pilgrimages undertaken by his readers to East Anglia or the East End of London on the trail of Austerlitz, let alone the introduction of the 'Sebald footpath' which follows the trail of the narrator in *Vertigo*, walking from the Austrian Oberjoch Pass down to his native village of Wertach in the Allgäu.

His touchstone book, *The Rings of Saturn*, was the subject of both a stage production in Cologne by the British director Katie Mitchell and a disappointing adaptation for the screen. In *Patience (After Sebald)* the film-maker Grant Gee does not do justice to the book, except for those atmospheric sequences that show grainy handy-cam tracking shots of country lanes on which the narrator walked in the text. The film features interviews with a cast of Anglophone writers and artists. Many of them seem to lack crucial contextual knowledge about Sebald, neglecting that his writings can only be properly understood in German and against his German cultural background.

While *Patience (After Sebald)* is probably the best-known example of homage gone wrong, it is tempting to speculate what Sebald would have made of the tribute concert that Patti Smith played in early 2011 at Snape Maltings, Suffolk. The American singer, who is also an accomplished poet, read several excerpts from Michael Hamburger's translation of *After Nature* and played a number of her greatest songs. It was a spellbinding evening, fusing furious rock'n'roll with Sebald's melancholic poetry and was a passionate and unusual way to pay tribute to his work (despite the fact that he certainly never really had any interest in punk rock).

Curious, if not to say bizarre, is the posthumous appropriation of his literary work by the art world. Many artists have cited Sebald as a source of inspiration. That is fair enough in itself; however, looking at the results, one must often wonder if it is rather a matter of associating mediocre art with a shining literary name. What would surely have astounded Sebald even more, are the endeavours by art theorists to declare him to be primarily a visual artist, in a truly ill-conceived attempt to demote his fiction to a mere addendum to his image material.[3]

*

The assumption that his books were originally written in English is another myth shared by many Anglophone readers. Given that he lived on English soil for more than three decades, it may seem only natural to have appropriated Sebald as an English writer. Interviewers were therefore regularly surprised when, unlike his idols Conrad and Nabokov, he expressed his resistance to changing his linguistic coat. 'Moving from one language to another, generally, entails giving up your first language,'[4] Sebald stated, and this was a sacrifice he was unwilling to make; despite all his reservations against his native land, he declared his loyalty to German, because 'I am attached to that language' (*EM* 69). Moreover, as his colleague Arthur Williams has correctly argued, 'the multi-layered precision of his language is inevitably at its richest and sharpest in the original German'.[5] An ambiguous title such as *Schwindel. Gefühle.*, for example, cannot be adequately rendered in English. This also applies to many of those liberally placed 'stumbling blocks' that aimed to perplex German readers. His (in)famous meandering sentences with their elaborate architecture are presented in dense blocks of text, unstructured by paragraphs (a style he borrowed from Thomas Bernhard, whom he greatly admired). These sentences are also rich in antiquated words and expressions that are strikingly unfamiliar to the majority of readers accustomed to standard German, since they are predominantly used in Austria and his native southern Germany. A case in point is the fact that characters with darker skin are regularly referred to in his books as 'Neger'. At least since the late 1970s, this politically incorrect word, which equates to negro in English, has been strictly banned from German public discourse and was subject to 'linguistic cleansing' campaigns which eliminated, for example, its appearance in popular children's books from the 1950s and 1960s. Sebald obviously does not use the term for racist reasons, but rather to hark back to an old-fashioned, and as it were 'innocent' use of language. Thus provocatively using a racist term in a non-racist way, Sebald subtly reminds his German readers of the way in which their native language has been tainted by the historical period of National Socialism. To Anglophone readers, this added element is inevitably lost in translation, which consistently renders the n-word innocuously as 'black person' or such like. That being said, Sebald was more than fortunate in his translators, Michael Hulse, Anthea Bell and Michael Hamburger, who all successfully transposed his complex and finely crafted German narratives into fluid English. Nonetheless, the resulting texts were not entirely the translators' work. Sebald engaged in intensive exchange with them about many details, often changing certain aspects for poetic reasons.[6]

Less well known is the fact that Sebald's indispensable assistant in this matter was his departmental secretary Beryl Ranwell (1932–2013), who according to Sebald had 'a good ear for English – which I certainly don't'.[7] Together they spent long hours reviewing the draft translations, and Ranwell advised Sebald on the use of English by everyday speakers of the language. The resulting texts, due to the author's heavy involvement, may be viewed as 'approved' English versions of the original German. Nevertheless, the full complexity, depth of allusion, and elegiac eloquence of Sebald's unique style can truly be experienced only in the original, as stated in the introduction to a recent English-language collection of essays on Sebald.[8]

It goes without saying that the divide between the two languages spoken by Sebald (as well as his more than practicable French) is also reflected in his personal position, torn between his country of birth and his country of residence. It makes sense in this context to bring up the German concept of *Heimat* which cannot be adequately translated into English, as it combines the attachment to one's geographical roots with a spiritual sense of belonging. Although Sebald had left Germany because of an acute sense of not feeling at home there, his adopted country never became a new *Heimat* for him. ' "I don't feel at home here in any sense", he said of Norwich, where he lived for thirty years' (*EM* 166). Despite his prototypical English lifestyle in his lovingly restored Old Rectory, Sebald never became 'one of us': 'In theory I could have had a British passport years ago. But I was born in a particular historical context, and I don't really have an option' (*EM* 69), he explained in an interview. His German origin was a burden in that sense: 'I feel you can't simply abdicate and say, well, it's nothing to do with me. I have inherited that backpack and I have to carry it, whether I like it or not' (*EM* 51).

Once a German, always a German, one is tempted to say. But Germany was no longer an option for Sebald. When he tried to resettle there in the mid-1970s, he returned disillusioned. Similarly, his trips back home hardly rekindled any feelings of belonging: 'I still suffer from homesickness, of course. I take the train from Munich, and it turns the corner southwards, near Kempten, and I feel [...] and then as soon as I get out of the railway station I want to go back. I can't stand the sight of it' (*EM* 67). Note the telling gap in this statement as Sebald tries to find the right words for his ambivalent feelings. In his books, the narrators usually find more uncompromising and critical words when talking about Germany. But the diatribes against the 'fatherland' all too evidently betray the deep sense of regret that 'home' no longer exists, neither here nor there. The only *Heimat* left for Sebald was his native language, and also the often painful labour which he devoted to writing his remarkable texts.

*

Anglophone readers deserve the credit for having discovered more quickly than their German counterparts the 'literary greatness' (in Susan Sontag's words) of Sebald's books. In one respect, however, he is not as unique as his English-speaking readers have assumed: his mix of words and images, though not widespread, is not uncommon in German letters. It recalls, for example, the work of Alexander Kluge, an admired author of (semi-)documentary fiction in Germany; or Hans Magnus Enzensberger's prose poem *Der Untergang der Titanic* (*The Sinking of the Titanic*, 1978); or the richly illustrated books of the academic outsider and cultural critic Klaus Theweleit, all of whom have to be regarded as well-known precursors and models in Germany. Sebald admired Theweleit's books not least because he was himself a sort of academic outsider. Throughout his career he was truly an unusual scholar, making it a point to distance himself polemically from mainstream *Germanistik*. Therefore, it comes as no surprise that he generated a considerable body of opponents both amongst the members of his discipline and also in literary circles. This is reflected by the fact that only one or two of the German literary prizes he received during his lifetime were major ones.

A particular case in point is Sebald's 1990 appearance at the Bachmann Literary Contest in Klagenfurt, Austria. Due to live television coverage, this is the most high-profile literary competition in the German-speaking world. Sebald read the Paul Bereyter story from *The Emigrants*, the very book that propelled him into literary stardom in its English translation. In Klagenfurt, however, he received none of the six prizes handed out by the jury, which consisted of leading academics and critics. Later, at the most important literary television show in Germany, *Das literarische Quartett* (*The Literary Quartet*), *The Emigrants* was savaged by Marcel Reich-Ranicki, host of the show and for many decades the most influential literary critic in Germany. He dismissed the book as literature discernibly written by an academic, therefore implying it was of no interest for general readers. Apart from being a misjudgement, as it turned out, the accusation highlighted Sebald's precarious status between the worlds of literature and academia. Needless to say,

111

some of his German Studies colleagues viewed his ascent to literary stardom with envy and suspicion. Equally, a fellow writer such as Günter Grass never forgave Sebald for attacking Alfred Döblin – Grass's literary model and 'teacher' – in his controversial study from 1980. The Nobel laureate Grass was certainly not the only one harbouring misgivings about Sebald in the German literary scene. Other well-known German authors have publicly criticized Sebald, mostly because of the confrontational nature of his critical writings. One telling fact clearly reveals the influence of his opponents: while Sebald was already on the short list for the Nobel Prize, he had even never been given the esteemed Georg Büchner Prize, which is awarded annually by the German Academy for Language and Literature. In the end, Sebald died before receiving either of these two well-deserved accolades.

The critical writings, many of which still await translation into English, provide an on-going bone of contention for the reception of Sebald in Germany. The essays collected in *The Natural History of Destruction* particularly attracted the scorn of the Germany literary establishment. In his Zurich lectures on *Air War and Literature*, delivered during the autumn of 1997, Sebald made bold claims that caused an immense uproar beyond the literary pages of the major national newspapers. Though his main point was fairly straightforward, his argument was much more complex than most of his critics initially comprehended.

Sebald castigated the failure of post-war German writers to adequately describe the Allied air raids on the German civil population and the destruction of many German cities, small and large alike. This accusation was dismissed initially as an oversimplification; as the ensuing discussion proved, however, Sebald had touched on a sore point regarding German politics of memory. Over the next few years, the debate he had provoked generated a plethora of historiographical books, academic conferences and popular accounts of the air war. Even forgotten novels that dealt with the atrocities committed by the British and US bomber commands, which had been out of print for ages, were suddenly resurrected.[9]

Similarly, Sebald was made into a bogeyman in 1993 following the publication of his polemical essay entitled *Between the Devil and the Deep Blue Sea. Alfred Andersch. Das Verschwinden in der Vorsehung (Between the Devil and the Deep Blue Sea. On AA,* in: NHD 107–46) in which he attacked the writer for his personal conduct during the Nazi era: amongst other things, Andersch divorced his Jewish wife in 1943, to meet Nazi requirements for publishing under their regime. Then a couple of years later, when he was held in a US POW camp, Andersch exploited his former marriage to obtain privileges. Similarly, he had made false claims about a number of biographical details relating, for example, to a term of imprisonment at the Dachau concentration camp in March 1933, or to his desertion from the Nazi army in June 1944. Sebald violently attacked Andersch on moral grounds and called for a complete dismissal of his literary works, as the opportunistic writer had always claimed his books were entirely based on truth. This highly exaggerated claim had elevated Andersch into a position of moral and literary authority, and he had become a much-admired literary figurehead of German post-war literature.[10] Sebald's iconoclasm – for it was this as much as a character assassination – aimed to uncover a malaise that he viewed as paradigmatic for post-war German literature: the chasm between what had actually happened and was witnessed by the writers on the one hand, and how they chose to write about it on the other, often concealing the truth while pretending to deliver an accurate account of the (Nazi) past.

Sebald's general animosity towards the established champions of post-war literature enraged many of their supporters and, in turn, created an animosity against his books. Others, who supported Sebald's literary works, found themselves in a dilemma: they had to underplay or blatantly ignore the existence of his highly problematic essays; for example, his polemic attack on the Jewish Holocaust survivor Jurek Becker only appeared posthumously, nearly two decades after it had been written.[11] Indeed, it is somewhat difficult to reconcile Sebald's pronounced criticism of German-Jewish writers, such as Carl Sternheim, Alfred Döblin and Jurek Becker, with his empathetic portrayal of (semi-)fictional Jewish biographies in books like *The Emigrants* or *Austerlitz*.

Sebald was more than once at odds with received wisdom, rules of political correctness and the prescribed views of German history. In his last German interview, published posthumously, he directly challenged the first commandment of political discourse in Germany, namely the uniqueness of the Holocaust: 'I do not at all perceive the disaster wrought by the Germans, as horrendous as it was, as a unique event – it had developed, with a certain consequentiality, from within European history'.[12] Again, this is not quite what one might expect from a writer who was glorified as the long-awaited restorer of the German-Jewish cultural symbiosis. But then, the very contradictory nature of Sebald's writings serves as a reminder that he was a far more complex figure than is often assumed. A patent dimension of waywardness and self-will exists that cannot, and indeed should not be exorcized.

*

The cult of Sebald that was already emerging during his lifetime has grown steadily since his death. 'Sebald is implicitly part of a long tradition of famous authorial deaths: Kleist, Celan, Kafka, Levi', according to one critic.[13] A truly remarkable literary lineage: three suicides, three Jews, two Holocaust survivors – Sebald, however, belonged in none of the above categories. Placing stones on his grave, as is customary in Judaism, won't change the fact that – despite rumours to the contrary – he is not of a hidden Jewish descent. Sebald was neither an unabashed philo-Semite nor a Zionist.[14] And he certainly never aimed to become what US critic Richard Eder declared him to be in his review of *Austerlitz*, namely the 'prime speaker of the Holocaust',[15] even though he had written about it with deep pain, grief and empathy in some of his books. More than once, he was cast into the role of redeemer – Saint Sebald, Max the Messiah. And don't forget about 'Sebald the Good German'. In his *Sebald Memorial Lecture* given in London in 2010, the writer Will Self correctly highlighted the self-congratulatory manner in which Sebald was claimed by the cultural establishment in the UK:

> In England, Sebald's one-time presence among us – even if we would never be so crass as to think this, let alone articulate it – is registered as further confirmation that we won, and won because of our righteousness, our liberality, our inclusiveness and our tolerance. Where else could the Good German have sprouted so readily?

Sebald, to reiterate, would have been appalled by all the distorting idolization and misguided veneration. Being a modest person, he abhorred adoration and accepted personal praise for his work with a good degree of shyness and embarrassment. While the vast majority of literary writers would have been delighted about academic recognition of their work, Sebald in November 2001 politely declined the invitation to appear at the first academic conference devoted to his writings. All too clearly, he may well have feared that this accolade marked the inauguration of what has rightly been labelled the 'Sebald industry', a voluminous, rapidly growing array of criticism that surrounds and often clouds his work. But the extent to which the burgeoning interest in his work has mushroomed since his premature death, it is safe to say, would have taken him quite by surprise. Similarly, he would be amazed by the fact that he now ranks as the equal of authors such as Peter Weiss or Thomas Bernhard, about whom he had written critical essays, and who later were very important for his own literary writing.

It is an astonishing story in any case: a *Germanist* outsider, who left behind his rural Bavarian background to become an unruly academic in England, has been turned into one of the most celebrated writers of the late twentieth century. An odd but somehow also very fitting trajectory for the man who was Winfried Georg Sebald.

Postscript

When you grow up promises are held up in front of you. Get your O levels done and your A levels and then everything will be fine. And then you do your BA and your PhD, but the more you are lured along this road, the more is taken away from you, the less the scope becomes. Day by day you leave things behind, ultimately your health, and so loss becomes the most common experience we have. I think somehow this has to be accounted for and as there are few other places where it is accounted for it has to be done by writing. It is quite clear to me that many people can identify with this view of life. It is not necessarily a pessimistic one; it is just a matter of fact that somehow this whole process is one in which you get done out of what you thought was your entitlement.

W. G. Sebald, 12 January 2001

Notes

CHAPTER 1. W. G. SEBALD: EMIGRANT AND ACADEMIC

1. For a more detailed discussion see Schütte, 'Out of the Shadows' in *Times Higher Education* 2017 (2011), 44–7.
2. The letter that informed him about the success of his application had initially ended up in the rubbish bin where Sebald had chucked it, wrongly assuming it was junk mail from a well-known Swiss food corporation. It was his wife who salvaged it from the bin.
3. Chris Bigsby, *Remembering and Imagining the Holocaust* (Cambridge: CUP, 2006), 31.
4. Maya Jaggi 'Recovered Memories' in *The Guardian* (22 September 2001).
5. W. G. Sebald/Tess Jaray, *For Years Now* (London: Short Book, 2001), 42.
6. See Philippa Comber, *Ariadne's Thread. In Memory of W. G. Sebald* (Norwich: Propolis, 2014), 43.
7. St Jerome Lecture 2001, W. G. Sebald in conversation with Maya Jaggi in *In Other Words. The Journal for Literary Translators* 21 (1997), 5–18, 11. Sebald would later 'recreate' this confrontation by inserting the picture of dead bodies in a forest in *The Rings of Saturn*, purportedly taken by one Major George Wyndham Le Strange.
8. Ray Furness on Sebald in a letter to Richard Sheppard, see *SM* 82.
9. A PDF of the typescript can be downloaded from http://ethos.bl.uk.
10. The literal translation of the title is *Air War and Literature*, the differing title of the English version was used at Sebald's request.
11. 'Characters, Plot, Dialogue? That's Not Really My Style', in *The Observer* (7 June 1980).
12. Thanks to my sustained efforts to interest radio stations in it, a radio play version was eventually produced by the WDR in Cologne and broadcast on 11 July 2015.

13. Though I am using the English titles of Sebald's books in this chapter, I refer to the German originals, giving their year of publication.
14. There are also parts of the project to be found in the 2008 exhibition catalogue *Wandernde Schatten. W. G. Sebalds Unterwelt* that are not yet translated into English.
15. See *Times Literary Supplement*, (29 November 1996), 15.
16. On the occasion, Sebald gave a personal and touching acceptance speech which can be found in *CS* 207–08.
17. See Michael Sanderson: *The History of the University of East Anglia Norwich* (Continuum: London, 2002).
18. For more details see *EM* 163–5.

CHAPTER 2. *AFTER NATURE* (1988)

1. The Graz-based *Manuskripte* was the literary mouthpiece of the young avant-garde movement during the Sixties and Seventies. Sebald had already published a number of critical essays in the journal, mostly on marginal writers to whom he felt particularly close (e.g. the schizophrenic poet Ernst Herbeck and the autodidact Herbert Achternbusch).
2. He received only a small number of reviews in major papers after its publication in autumn 1988, but in 1991 was the first recipient of the Fedor-Malchow Prize for nature poetry; although a minor and soon discontinued literary prize, its award was an encouraging achievement for Sebald.
3. Rüdiger Görner, 'After Words. On W. G. Sebald's Poetry' in Görner (ed.), *The Anatomist of Melancholy. Essays in Memory of W. G. Sebald*, (Munich: Iudicium, 2003), 75–80, 76.
4. See Eric L. Santner's *On Creaturely Life. Rilke, Benjamin, Sebald* (Chicago: University of Chicago Press, 2009).

CHAPTER 3. *VERTIGO* (1990)

1. Maya Jaggi, 'Recovered memories' in *The Guardian*, (22 September 2001).
2. Sebald did indeed travel to Italy in the first week of August 1987, staying in Venice, Milan, Verona and Riva.
3. Helen Finch, *Sebald's Bachelors. Queer Resistance and the Unconforming Life* (Oxford: Legenda 2013), 92.
4. Translated quote from Sebald's Kafka essay 'Tiere, Menschen, Maschinen. Zu Kafkas Evolutionsgeschichten' in *Literatur & Kritik*

205/6 (1986), 194–201, 198.

5. The original German version was published in 1986 in the Austrian journal *Literatur & Kritik*.
6. Daniel Medin, *Three Sons. Franz Kafka and the Fiction of J. M. Coetzee, Philip Roth, and W. G. Sebald* (Evanston: Northwestern University Press, 2010), 132.

CHAPTER 4. *THE EMIGRANTS* (1992)

1. Vintage edition, the German edition by Fischer equally talks incorrectly about 'four Jews expelled from their European homeland'.
2. This expression, introduced with the Nuremberg Race Laws of 1935, was meant to indicate that one of his four grandparents was of Jewish descent.
3. In reality, Müller made two suicide attempts; the first, unsuccessful one, took place at roughly the place depicted on the photo; the second attempt then happened at a different location, in the opposite direction of the tracks shown on the photograph.
4. Sebald's moving essay on Hebel opens his collection *A Place in the Country* from 1998.
5. See the article 'Ein ideenreicher Pädagoge. Armin Müller feiert in Sonthofen seinen 70. Geburtstag, in *Allgäuer Anzeigeblatt*, (22 December 1980).
6. Originally called Max Aurach, Sebald changed the name of the character to Ferber for the English version, following the protest by Auerbach who felt that his biography and two illustrations were used without permission.
7. See Sebald, *Die Beschreibung des Unglücks*, 11.

CHAPTER 5. *THE RINGS OF SATURN* (1995)

1. In this case, however, Sebald changed the name for the English translation; his actual name was Alec Garrard and he appears as such in the German original.
2. Later on there is a touching episode in which the narrator strokes a sleeping pig on a field 'till at length it sighed like one enduring endless suffering' (*RS* 66).
3. The clipping is widely held to be a fabrication by Sebald as it cannot be traced back to the local newspaper. Also, there are no records of a Major Le Strange in any of the available registers. On the other hand, there is no evidence indicating it to be a forgery. It is highly

unlikely that Sebald had the means to create an image so closely resembling an authentic newspaper article.

4. Thereby, it needs to be stressed here, they come astonishingly close to the gratuitous depictions of violence that Sebald so vehemently criticized in Döblin's novels.

5. For fairness' sake, it should be added that while Sebald's descriptions of the atrocities committed during the rebellion are by and large according to historical truth, his very negative portrayal of the Empress paints an overly distorted picture of her.

6. Worth mentioning here is the fact that while Hamburger was married to the English poet Anne Beresford, Sebald's wife had an Austrian background so he spent his domestic life speaking German.

7. Walter Benjamin, *Illuminations. Essays and Reflections* (London: Pimlico, 2011), 258.

CHAPER 6. *AUSTERLITZ* (2001)

1. James Wood pointed this out already in 2011 though without questioning Sebald's claims about the existence of the supposed colleague: 'The photograph of the little boy in his cape is even more poignant. I have read reviews of this book that suggest it is a photograph of the young Sebald – such is our desire, I suppose, not to let the little boy pass into orphaned anonymity. But the photograph is not of the young Sebald; I came across it in Sebald's literary archive at Marbach, outside Stuttgart, and discovered just an ordinary photographic postcard, with, on the reverse side, "Stockport: 30p" written in ink.' James Wood: 'Sent East', in *London Review of Books* 33/19 (2011), 15–18, 17.

2. The question regarding whether the figure of Austerlitz is based on other models is a bone of contention amongst Sebald scholars. Sebald himself named Ludwig Wittgenstein as a model. Lynne Wolff makes a case for Saul Friedlander due to biographical similarities (Wolff: *W. G. Sebald's Hybrid Poetics*, 136–7) and some traits of Austerlitz also point to the poet Franz Wurm, who was born in Prague, as well as to a UEA colleague of Sebald.

3. Worth pointing out here is the fact that Sebald's mother was also called Rosa; the title of Bechhöfer's memoir must hence have struck a special chord with him.

4. Bechhöfer wrote to me: 'Whilst I consider this work to be a masterpiece on the subject of displacement and how it really feels, I would have appreciated some consultation. Due to the use of my book, an acknowledgement of this, I continue to believe, is

required.' (Email dated 18 May 2015.)

5. Wittgenstein's eyes are also gazing at the reader of *Austerlitz* on page 3 of the book, paired with the eyes of Sebald's friend, the artist Jan Peter Tripp. Sebald had a special interest in Wittgenstein and it is an odd, possibly meaningful coincidence that the three syllables of his spirit brother's surname equate to Sebald's own initials.

6. Contrary to what is often assumed, the rucksack on the photo on page 55 belonged not to Sebald but a friend, the poet Stephen Watts.

7. Jacobson was unaware that Sebald has used his book in the coda of *Austerlitz* and never had any personal contact with him.

CHAPTER 7. THE CULT OF SEBALD

1. For example, see Teju Cole's 2011 novel *Open City* which is clearly based on *The Rings of Saturn*. It features a Nigerian-German psychiatrist as a protagonist who perambulates through New York.

2. For an excellent blog also devoted to literature with embedded photographs, and to Sebald in particular, see Vertigo by Terry Pitts @ http://sebald.wordpress.com.

3. See Lise Patt (ed.), *Searching for Sebald. Photography after W. G. Sebald* (Los Angeles: Institute of Cultural Inquiry, 2007).

4. St Jerome Lecture 2001. W. G. Sebald in conversation with Maya Jaggi in *In Other Words. Journal For Literary Translators* 21 (2003), 5–18, 16.

5. Arthur Williams, 'W G. Sebald' in *The Literary Encyclopedia*, (24 April 2002).

6. On Sebald in translation see Arthur Williams, 'W. G. Sebald's Three-Letter Word. On the Parallel World of the English Translations' in Jeannette Baxter, Valerie Henitiuk, Ben Hutchinson (eds.), *A Literature of Restitution. Critical Essays on W. G. Sebald* (Manchester: Manchester University Press, 2013), 25–41.

7. See Gordon Turner, 'Beryl Ranwell Obituary' in *The Guardian*, (1 July 2013).

8. Jeanette Baxter, Valerie Henitiuk, Ben Hutchinson, 'Introduction' in Baxter, Henitiuk, Hutchinson (eds.), *A Literature of Restitution. Critical Essays on W. G. Sebald* (Manchester: Manchester University Press, 2013), 3.

9. Most importantly, Gert Ledig, *Payback* (London: Granta, 2003).

10. See Günter Grass's firm status as the 'moral consciousness' of German politics – until he admitted in 2006 to his membership in an SS army division during the final months of the war, a biographical detail he had kept under lock and key for sixty years.

11. I unsuccessfully offered the essay, which is contained among the papers in Sebald's estate, to a number of German literary magazines. Eventually, it was picked up by *Sinn und Form* who published it, to considerable media interest, in early 2010.
12. See Sebald, 'Mit einem kleinen Strandspaten Abschied von Deutschland nehmen', interview with Uwe Pralle in *Süddeutsche Zeitung*, (22 December 2001).
13. Scott Denham, 'Foreword. The Sebald Phenomenon' in Scott Denham, Mark R. McCulloh (eds.), *W .G. Sebald. History – Memory – Trauma* (Berlin: De Gruyter, 2006), 2.
14. When questioned about his position on Israel, he just said: 'The situation is deplorable, there's no question. But it's an issue I've avoided.' (Maya Jaggi, 'Recovered Memories' in *The Guardian* 22 September 2001).
15. Richard Eder, 'Excavating a Life' in *The New York Times Book Review* (28 October 2000), 10.

Primary Bibliography

SEBALD'S WORKS IN CHRONOLOGICAL ORDER

1969   *Carl Sternheim: Kritiker und Opfer der Wilhelminischen Ära*, revised MA dissertation

1980   *Der Mythus der Zerstörung im Werk Döblins*, German version of PhD thesis

1985   *Die Beschreibung des Unglücks. Zur österreichischen Literatur von Stifter bis Handke*, translation forthcoming by J. Catling

1988   *After Nature. (Nach der Natur. Ein Elementargedicht)*, translation by M. Hamburger, English ed. 2002

1990   *Vertigo. (Schwindel. Gefühle.)*, translation by M. Hulse, English ed. 1999

1991   *Unheimliche Heimat. Essays zur österreichischen Literatur*, translation forthcoming by J. Catling

1992   *The Emigrants. (Die Ausgewanderten. Vier lange Erzählungen)*, translation by M. Hulse, English ed. 1996

1995   *The Rings of Saturn. (Die Ringe des Saturn. Eine englische Wallfahrt)*, translation by M. Hulse, English ed. 1998

1998   *A Place in the Country. (Logis in einem Landhaus)*, translation by J. Catling, English ed. 2013

1999   *On the Natural History of Destruction. (Luftkrieg und Literatur)*, translation by A. Bell, English ed. 2003

2001   *Austerlitz*, translation by A. Bell. (German original appeared in February, English version in October)

2001   *For Years Now.* Poems by W. G. Sebald. Images by Tess Jaray

2003   *Unrecounted. 33 Poems (Unerzählt. 33 Texte)*, translation by M. Hamburger, English ed. 2004

2003   *Campo Santo. (Campo Santo. Prosa, Essays)*, translation by A. Bell, English ed. 2005

2008   *Across the Land and the Water. Selected Poems, 1964–2001. (Über das Land und das Wasser. Ausgewählte Gedichte 1964–2001)*, translation by I. Galbraith, English ed. 2011

Select Bibliography

The amount of criticism published on Sebald, not just in English and German, but also in French, Spanish, Italian, Scandinavian and other languages, is by now too vast to be surveyed by any one person. The following bibliographical references point the interested reader to indispensable sources of information and selected key works on Sebald in English.

HANDBOOKS

Saturn's Moons: W. G. Sebald – A Handbook, eds. Jo Catling, Richard Hibbitt (Oxford: Legenda, 2011)

W. G. Sebald-Handbuch: Leben – Werk – Wirkung, eds. Michael Niehaus, Claudia Öhlschläger (Metzler: Stuttgart, 2017)

INTRODUCTIONS

McCulloh, Mark R., *Understanding W. G. Sebald* (Columbia: University of South Carolina Press, 2003)

Schütte, Uwe, *W. G. Sebald. Einführung in Leben und Werk* (Stuttgart: UTB, 2011)

REVIEW ARTICLES

Long, J. J., 'W. G. Sebald: A Bibliographical Essay on Current Research' in *W. G. Sebald and the Writing of History*, eds. Anne Fuchs, J. J. Long (Würzburg: Königshausen & Neumann, 2007), 11–29

Sheppard, Richard, 'Woods, trees and the spaces in between': a Report on Work Published on W. G. Sebald 2005–2008, in *Journal of European Studies* 39 (2009), 79–128

Sheppard, Richard, 'Dexter – Sinister: Some Observations on Decrypting the Mors Code in the Work of W. G. Sebald' in *Journal of European Studies* 35 (2005), 419–63

Wolff, Lynne, 'Das metaphysische Unterfutter der Realität: Recent Publications and Trends in W. G. Sebald Research' in *Monatshefte* 99:1 (2007), 313–16

Zisselsberger, Markus, 'A Persistent Fascination: Recent Publications on the Work of W. G. Sebald 2005–2008' in *Monatshefte* 101:1 (2009), 88–105

EDITED VOLUMES AND SPECIAL EDITIONS OF JOURNALS

Baxter, Jeanette, Henitiuk, Valerie and Hutchinson, Ben (eds.), *A Literature of Restitution. Critical Essays on W. G. Sebald* (Manchester: Manchester University Press, 2013)

Denham, Scott and McCulloch, Mark (eds.), *W. G. Sebald: History – Memory – Trauma* (Berlin: De Gruyter, 2007)

Fischer, Gerald (ed.), *W. G. Sebald: Schreiben ex Patria/Expatriate Writing* (Amsterdam: Rodopi, 2009), includes chapters in English

Görner, Rüdiger (ed.), *The Anatomist of Melancholy: Essays in Memory of W. G. Sebald*, (Munich: Iudicium, 2003)

Long, J. J. and Whitehead, Anne (eds.), *W. G. Sebald. A Critical Companion* (Edinburgh: Edinburgh University Press, 2004)

Patt, Lise (ed.), *Searching for Sebald. Photography after W. G. Sebald* (Los Angeles: Institute of Cultural Inquiry, 2007)

Schütte, Uwe (ed.), *Über W. G. Sebald: Beiträge zu einem anderen Bild des Autor* (Berlin: De Gruyter, 2016), includes chapters in English

Sheppard, Richard (ed.), *Journal of European Studies* 41: 3–4 (2011), W. G. Sebald Special Issue

Zisselsberger, Markus (ed.), *The Undiscover'd Country: W. G. Sebald and the Poetics of Travel* (Rochester, NY: Camden House, 2010)

MONOGRAPHS AND PHD THESES

Blackler, Deane, *Reading W. G. Sebald: Adventure and Disobedience* (Rochester: Camden House, 2007)

Etzler, Melissa S., *Writing from the Periphery: W. G. Sebald and Outsider Art* (PhD thesis, University of California, Berkeley, 2014)

Hutchins, Michael D., *Tikkun: W. G. Sebald's Melancholy Messianism* (PhD thesis, McMicken College of Arts and Sciences, Cincinnati, 2011)

Long, J. J., *W. G. Sebald: Image, Archive, Modernity* (Edinburgh: Edinburgh University Press, 2007)

Santner, Eric L., *On Creaturely Life: Rilke, Benjamin, Sebald* (Chicago: University of Chicago Press, 2006)

Wolff, Lynn, *W. G. Sebald's Hybrid Poetics. Literature as Historiography* (Berlin: De Gruyter, 2014)

INTERVIEWS

Hoffmann, Torsten (ed.), *Auf ungeheuer dünnem Eis. Gespräche 1971 bis 2001* (Frankfurt: Fischer, 2011)

Kafatou, Sarah, 'An Interview with W. G. Sebald' in *Harvard Review* 15 (1998), 31–5

Mühling, Jens, 'The Permanent Exile of W. G. Sebald' in *Pretext* 7 (2003), 15–26

Schwartz, Lynne Sharon (ed.), *The Emergence of Memory. Conversations with W. G. Sebald* (New York: Seven Stories, 2007)

EXHIBITION CATALOGUE

Bülow, Ulrich, Gfrereis, Heike and Strittmatter, Ellen (eds.), *Wandernde Schatten: W. G. Sebalds Unterwelt* (Marbach: DLA, 2008)

WEB SOURCES

Vertigo (Terry Pitts)
http://sebald.wordpress.com

W. G. Sebald (Christian Wirth)
http://www.wgsebald.de

FILMS

Patience (After Sebald). Director, Grant Gee, 2011. (90 mins)

W. G. Sebald. The Emigrant. Director, Thomas Honickel, 2007, English subtitles, (45 mins)

Index